ATTENTION DEFICIT HYPERACTIVITY AND LEARNING DISORDERS

QUESTIONS AND ANSWERS

J. GORDON MILLICHAP, M.D., F.R.C.P.

*Pediatric Neurologist,
Children's Memorial Hospital;
Northwestern University Medical School,
Chicago, Illinois*

PNB • Publishers
Chicago

Published and Distributed Throughout the World by
PNB • Publishers
P.O. Box 11391
Chicago, Illinois 60611, U.S.A.

Printed in the U.S.A.

ISBN 0-9629115-4-2
Library of Congress Catalog Card Number: 98-91663

Reprinted 1999

In tribute to

Nancy

PREFACE

ADHD, or attention deficit hyperactivity disorder, is a syndrome commonly encountered in children and adolescents, and occasionally in adults. It is often associated with learning disabilities, resulting in failure to achieve the expected level of academic performance. At least one child in every classroom and approximately 3 to 5% of the school age population is inattentive and hyperactive. The cause is diverse and often undetermined; genetic and environmental factors have been invoked in some cases. A family member, either parent or sibling, has a history of ADHD in 20 to 30%, and minor anomalies of brain development, premature birth and anoxic injury, infection, and toxic lead exposure are some of the presumed causes. A neurologic basis for ADHD is supported by reports of MRI evidence of structural brain abnormalities, and subtle signs of immature brain development on neurologic examination.

Hyperactivity may be recognized by the parents soon after birth or when the child begins to walk, but the diagnosis is frequently delayed until a teacher observes the inability to focus, distractibility, and restless behavior in the classroom. An initial evaluation by the pediatrician or family physician is usually followed by consultations with the pediatric neurologist or psychiatrist, a psychological evaluation, and laboratory investigations when indicated.

Treatment consists of educational accommodations, medications, behavior modification, and family counselling. Central nervous stimulants have a remarkable beneficial effect in 80% of ADHD children, helping them to focus, reducing distractibility and restless behavior, and facilitating learning and memory. Used intermittently in conservative doses, as an aid to education, and monitored closely by a physician, stimulant medications are free from serious side effects. Alternative therapies, including diet, and visual and auditory training, may be supportive but rarely having the immediate and measurable effects of pharmacotherapy.

This book is written for the concerned parent and informed layman, the interested teacher and student, the psychologist, and pediatrician. The questions are those most frequently asked by parents and teachers who care for the hyperactive child with attention deficit and learning disorders. The answers are supported when possible by published results of controlled studies. The format is both simple and more detailed, with statements of facts, scientific data, and results of original research provided in small print for those interested. References are listed for all publications.

The reader should be able to evaluate the current extent of our knowledge of causes, diagnosis, treatment methods, and outcome of children with ADHD and learning disorders. Comorbid tics, Tourette syndrome, seizures, headaches, and oppositional, conduct and compulsive disorders are also covered. It is hoped that the questions and answers will lead to a better understanding of the child with ADHD and improvement in the medical, educational, and psychological management.

J. Gordon Millichap, M.D.

ACKNOWLEDGMENTS

My patients, many of whom have overcome or outgrown their attention deficits and are leading successful adult lives, and their parents, who cared for and supported them through difficult times, are the inspiration for this book. My colleagues and friends, Terry Finn and Rosemary Egan have provided expert neuropsychological evaluations and child and family counselling, without which the medical management of my patients with ADHD would be incomplete and less effective. My son, Martin Millichap, clinical psychologist, and my colleague, Charles Swisher, pediatric neurologist, read early versions of the text and made constructive suggestions. My late wife, Nancy Millichap, author of a book on dyslexia, encouraged me to continue an interest in attention deficit and learning disorders.

I am indebted to all.

J. Gordon Millichap

TABLE OF CONTENTS

ATTENTION DEFICIT HYPERACTIVITY AND LEARNING DISORDERS

QUESTIONS AND ANSWERS

CHAPTER 1

WHAT IS ADHD?

A DHD, the abbreviation for **Attention-Deficit/Hyperactivity Disorder**, is the name coined by doctors to describe children, adolescents, and even some adults, who are inattentive, easily distracted, abnormally overactive, and impulsive in their behavior. ADHD is a "syndrome" in medical terms, meaning a collection of symptoms which frequently occur together. It is not a "disease" with a specific known cause, like diabetes or pneumonia; it cannot be treated, controlled, or cured with a specific hormone or an antibiotic.

Many different factors have been suggested as the cause of ADHD, and the treatment requires several different approaches, involving medical, neuropsychological, educational, and parental disciplines. It is sometimes called a "heterogeneous" disorder, meaning a mixture of symptom-complexes with a variety of different causes.

Q: How long has ADHD been recognized?

A: Under different names, the syndrome of ADHD has been recognized for more than a century. It is not a new diagnosis or a reflection of this 20th century, competitive and fast moving society. In the nineteenth century, Heinrich Hoffman (1809-1874), a German physician and poet, wrote about "Fidgety Philip" who couldn't sit still. The poem portrays the typical behavior of a child with ADHD, living in times when children were subject to discipline less permissive than at present. A stricter control of behavior did not appear to prevent the occurrence of the hyperkinetic syndrome.

Medical references to a similar childhood behavioral syndrome date back to the beginning of the century, with articles published in the British journal, *Lancet* (1902, 1904) and the *Journal of the American Medical Association* (1921). Behavioral abnormalities were associated with head injury in the earliest reports, and they occurred as a complication of encephalitis following the World War I influenza epidemic of 1918.

The similarities of the hyperkinetic behavior following head trauma and that described in children recovering from encephalitis were described in later articles (Hohman, Ebaugh, 1922; Strecker, Ebaugh, 1924). These authors found the children distractible as well as overactive. "Organic drivenness" was a term used to describe the behavioral disturbance following epidemic encephalitis, and damage to the lower brain structures, or brainstem, was suggested as the underlying cause. (Kahn, Cohen, 1934).

This description of behavioral symptoms caused by brain disease or injury was followed by a variety of reports of behavioral syndromes having similar characteristics that were linked to brain damage or dysfunction.

Q: What are some of the alternative labels previously used to describe children with ADHD?

A: Many different terms have been used to describe the hyperactive child with attention deficits and learning disorders. Some have emphasized the symptoms (hyperactivity, inattentiveness), some refer to the presumed cause (brain damage or dysfunction), and others the educational problems (perception and learning disorders) associated with the behavior. The list of names for this syndrome is long, close to forty, and the following are some examples:
- The hyperactive child syndrome.
- The hyperkinetic syndrome.
- The brain-injured child.
- Minimal brain dysfunction.
- The perceptually handicapped child.
- Learning disabled child.

None of these terms is entirely satisfactory because the symptoms and causes of the syndrome are many and variable. Hyperactivity is the most common and striking complaint, but some children have normal or even lesser degrees of activity, the syndrome expressed mainly by inattentiveness and distractibility. Subtle neurological abnormalities, perception deficits, and learning disabilities are frequently associated but not invariable findings. The current term ADHD emphasizes the symptoms but minimizes the importance of possible underlying causes and associated learning problems.

Q: How has the present concept of ADHD evolved and changed over the last 75 years?

A: From the initial descriptions and concept of a brain damage syndrome, beginning with *"postencephalitic behavior disorder,"* in 1922, proceeding to the *"brain-injured child"* (1947) and the *"perceptually handicapped child"* (1963), and ending with *"minimal brain dysfunction,"* in 1966, the emphasis turned to symptoms, when the American Psychiatric Association included the syndrome in their Diagnostic and Statistical Manual (DSM) in 1968.

The first entry of the syndrome in DSM-II (1968) used the term *"hyperkinetic reaction of childhood or adolescence."* In 1980, the DSM-III recognized two subtypes of a syndrome of *"attention deficit disorder (ADD)"* - *"ADD with hyperactivity"* and *"ADD without hyperactivity."* In 1987, the DSM-III was revised (DSM-III-R) and the term *"attention-deficit hyperactivity disorder (ADHD)"* was used. Finally, in 1994, the DSM-IV now recognizes three subtypes of the syndrome: *"ADHD-inattentive type,"* *"ADHD-hyperactive-impulsive type,"* and *"ADHD-combined type."* A minimum number of criteria are required for the diagnosis of each subtype.

Q: What are the criteria required for the diagnosis of these subtypes of ADHD?

A: (1) ADHD *"Inattentive"* subtype, without hyperactivity. (Code 314.00) At least six of the following nine symptoms have been noted for at least six months and are often present during school or play activities;

1. Makes careless mistakes;
2. Can't maintain attention;
3. Doesn't listen when spoken to;
4. Fails to finish tasks;
5. Seems disorganized;
6. Avoids tasks;
7. Loses things;
8. Easily distracted;
9. Forgetful.

(2) ADHD *"Hyperactive-Impulsive"* subtype. (Code 314.01) Six (or more) of the following symptoms have been present for at least six months:

Hyperactivity:
1. Fidgety;
2. Leaves seat in classsroom or at dinner table;
3. Runs or climbs excessively;
4. Can't play quietly;
5. Always "on the go;"
6. Talks a lot.
Impulsivity:
7. Blurts out answers to questions;
8. Can't wait in line or take turn;
9. Often interrupts.

(3) ADHD *"Combined* " type.
Criteria for both the *"Inattentive"* and the *"Hyperactive-Impulsive"* types have been present for at least six months.

The term *"In Partial Remission"* is applied to older children and adolescents whose symptoms have lessened with age or treatment and no longer add up to the required number for diagnosis.

Q: How is the diagnosis of ADHD made?

A: The typical diagnostic symptoms of **Attention-Deficit/Hyperactivity Disorder** are a persistent pattern of inattention and/or hyperactivity and impulsiveness of an abnormal severity and frequency. Symptoms should have been present before age 7 years, they should be observed in at least two settings (school, home, work-place, or doctor's office), and are sufficient to impair academic, social, or occupational functions. The symptoms cannot be explained by a mental illness such as depression, anxiety, or personality disorder.

Questionnaires completed by parents, school teachers, psychologists, and physicians are used in arriving at the diagnosis. A neurological examination that uncovers signs of brain dysfunction or damage of a subtle type, and psychological tests showing deficits in perception and learning ability can be additional supportive evidence, although these findings are not essential for the diagnosis of ADHD. A specific chemical or laboratory test is not available, but abnormal levels of lead in the blood, thyroid hormone imbalance, or certain chromosomal anomalies (fragile X disease) may rarely provide an explanation for the symptoms.

Q: Is ADHD really a medical deficit, or an excuse for social deviance in behavior?

A: Some skeptics argue that the symptoms of ADHD may be explained by a variation of "normal" behavior, a so-called boisterous child, or a reflection of our society. Sociologists criticize doctors for having "medicalized" symptoms that should be regarded as deviant behavior and an adaptation to the social environment (Conrad P, 1973, 1980).

The medical concept of deviant behavior has humanitarian benefits for the individual, allowing less condemnation and less social stigma among peers and adults. The child with a diagnosis of ADHD is no longer the "bad boy" of the classroom. He has an "illness," requiring regular visits to the nurse for medicine at lunchtime. The disruptive and distractible behavior is not his fault. The diagnosis of ADHD is even used as an excuse for conduct disorders and drug addiction, sometimes exerting pressure on the justice system and claiming undeserved leniency.

The medicalization of ADHD, according to the sociologists, has followed the availability of a treatment to control the deviant behavior. They infer that the syndrome would not be recognized as an illness, if the paradoxical, quietening effect of stimulant medications had not been discovered (Bradley, 1937). By defining ADHD as a medical problem, we may be diverting attention from the family, school or other factors in the social environment of probable underlying significance.

These arguments are an important reminder to physicians, parents, and teachers that the management of the child with ADHD must not rely exclusively on the prescription of stimulant or other medications. Treatment is "multimodal," including parental counselling, child behavior modification, and appropriate classroom size and teaching techniques, as well as medical intervention.

Q: How prevalent is ADHD? Is sex a factor?

A: Approximately 4% of children under 12 years of age are affected, or at least one in every classroom. Boys are affected three to six times more commonly than girls. Some authorities have estimated the prevalence as high as 10%, and even 20%, in school children between 5 and 12 years of age. One report claimed a total of 3 million children with ADHD in the United States.

ADHD is recognized worldwide, but the reported prevalence varies in different countries, with less than 1 in a 1000 in a study of 10- and 11-year-old children in the Isle of Wight, UK. (Rutter M et al, 1970) The accuracy and comparison of these statistics are affected by the age of the study population, the variability of the patient selection and the lack of agreement on the definition of diagnostic criteria.

In a recent study at Vanderbilt University, Nashville, TN, involving 8000 children in a Tennessee county, with ratings completed by 400 teachers, the estimates of prevalence of ADHD were higher when using the new diagnostic criteria listed in DSM-IV, as compared to DSM-III-R criteria. (Wolraich ML et al,

1996). Prevalence rates were 7% for ADHD using DSM-III-R, and 11% with DSM-IV criteria, an increase of 57%. The inattentive (AD) subtype of ADHD occurred in 5%, the hyperactive-impulsive (H-I) type in 2.5%, and the combined type in 3.5%. Boys outnumbered girls with a 4:1 ratio for the ADHD-HI and 2:1 for ADHD-AD.

Q: At what age do symptoms of ADHD begin?

A: According to the DSM-IV criteria for diagnosis of ADHD, some symptoms should be present before the age of seven years. Hyperactivity is recognized most commonly at about four or five years of age, when the child starts school, although many parents complain about excessive motor restlessness in infancy. In fact, some mothers have predicted the birth of a hyperactive child because of excessive fetal movements during pregnancy.

The environment will often influence the time of onset of symptoms. A child who is mildly restless at home or in the doctor's office may become hyperactive and distractible when entering a structured situation, such as a school classroom. On a one-to-one, student-teacher ratio, as in private tutoring, the child may function reasonably well, whereas in a large class of students, the symptoms of ADHD will immediately become apparent. Parents are sometimes dismayed at the reports from school, because in the home environment symptoms can be less obvious.

REFERENCES

American Psychiatric Association (APA): Diagnostic and

Statistical Manual of Mental Disorders. 4th ed. Washington, DC; APA;1994.

Bradley C. The behavior of children receiving Benzedrine. Am J Psychiatry 1937;94:577-585.

Conrad P. The discovery of hyperkinesis: Notes on the medicalization of deviant behavior. Soc Sci & Med 1973;7:12-21.

Conrad P, Schneider JW. Deviance and Medicalization. From badness to sickness. St Louis, Mo, CV Mosby, 1980.

Ebaugh F. Neuropsychiatric sequelae of acute epidemic encephalitis in children. Am J Dis Child 1923;25:89-97.

English T. The after effects of head injuries. Lancet 1904;1:485-489.

Hoffman H. Fidgety Philip. In: The Oxford Dictionary of Quotations, 2nd Ed. London, Oxford University Press, 1955.

Hohman LB. Post-encephalitic behavior disorders in children. Johns Hopkins Hospital Bulletin 1922;380:372-375.

Kahn E, Cohen L. Organic drivenness: A brain stem syndrome and experience. N Engl J Med 1934;210:748-756.

Leahly S, Sands I. Mental disturbances in children following epidemic encephalitis. JAMA 1921;76:373.

Rutter M, Tizard J, Whitmore K. Education, Health and Behavior. London, Longman, 1970.

Still GF. Some abnormal physical conditions in children. Lancet 1902;1:1008-12,1077-82,1163-68.

Strecker E, Ebaugh F. Neuropsychiatric sequelae of cerebral trauma in children. Arch Neurol Psychiatr 1924;12:443-453.

Wolraich ML et al. Comparison of diagnostic criteria for attention-deficit hyperactivity disorder in a county-wide sample. J Am Acad Child Adolesc Psychiatry 1996;35:319-324.

CHAPTER 2

WHAT CAUSES ADHD?

The causes of ADHD are many and varied, they are often only presumptive, and frequently no cause can be found. A disorder of unknown cause is referred to as *idiopathic,* and possibly genetic or environmental. A majority of cases of ADHD are idiopathic or of uncertain cause. A delay in development or maturation of the nervous system is sometimes proposed as an explanation for ADHD, especially in cases with mild or "soft" neurological deficits.

Causes are classified by their time of occurrence: 1) before birth (prenatal); 2) at or near the time of birth (neonatal); and 3) after birth (postnatal). They may also be a) genetic and familial, or b) acquired. Rarely, a chromosomal anomaly, fragile X disease, is the underlying cause of ADHD.

Prenatal causes include cerebral maldevelopments and arachnoid cysts, maternal anemia, toxemia of pregnancy, alcohol (fetal alcohol syndrome), cocaine abuse, and tobacco smoke. Other environmental factors sometimes suspected are exposure to lead, PCBs and pesticides in the water and diet. The season of birth may be a risk factor, and exposure to viral infections, especially influenza, in the first trimester of pregnancy or at the time of birth has been correlated with the diagnosis of ADHD.

Neonatal factors which may be causally related to ADHD are as follows: premature birth, breech delivery, birth asphyxia, anoxia or hemorrhage, with encephalopathy (brain damage). *Postnatally,* the infant may have suffered a head injury, meningitis, encephalitis, or low blood sugar. Drugs used to treat childhood illnesses, asthma and epilepsy, frequently cause or exacerbate hyperactive behavior and result in attention and learning deficits. The role of diet in the cause of ADHD is controversial, but the ingestion of food additives and sucrose, and allergies to certain foods are occasionally significant. A lack of iron in the diet and anemia are documented potential causes and rarely, thyroid hormone dysfunction is asociated with ADHD.

Hyperactivity and distractibility caused primarily by mood disorders, anxiety disorder, or personality disorder are excluded from the diagnostic classification of ADHD.

Q: What is the evidence for structural or functional brain changes and a neurological basis for ADHD?

A: The neurologic or anatomic theory of hyperactivity and ADHD is based on numerous experimental studies in animals, neurological and electroencephalographic (EEG) examinations of children, and magnetic resonance imaging (MRI) of the brain. Positron emission tomography (PET) studies, showing changes in glucose metabolism in the frontal lobes of the brain, point to a localized cerebral abnormality in adults who were hyperactive since childhood.

Neurologic "soft" signs, including motor impersistence (an inability to maintain postures or movements), distractibility (an inability to maintain attention), and attentional control and response inhibition, are indicative of right sided frontal cerebral lesions. Frontal cerebral lesions and their connections with the basal ganglia or striate cortex produce the greatest number and degree of hyperactive behavioral responses. The right prefrontal cortex has a role in attentional control and inhibiting responses, whereas the basal ganglia are involved in motor control and the execution of behavioral responses. Distractibility and impulsivity in ADHD children reflect deficits in response inhibition.

Injury or abnormal development of areas of the brain other than the frontal lobes may also be associated with the syndrome of ADHD and impairment of language and social skills. Cognitive dysfunction and ADHD are reported in children with temporal lobe lesions, and a connection with the fronto-striatal circuitry is possible in these cases.

At Duke University Medical Center, Durham, NC, deficits of cognitive function, language development, and social skills were reported in 4 children with bilateral medial temporal lobe (hippocampus) sclerosis, associated with severe epilepsy beginning in early childhood. MRI showed abnormal signals and 25% loss of hippocampal volume (DeLong GR, Heinz ER, 1997).

I have recently encountered a syndrome and cystic maldevelopment affecting the temporal lobe of the brain in 5 children with ADHD, and colleagues have since informed me of similar cases in their practices (Millichap JG, 1997). Although rare, the diagnosis of this association and syndrome points to the potential importance of prenatal factors in the cause of ADHD.

An MRI of the head of a case of the Temporal Lobe Arachnoid Cyst/ADHD (TLAC/ADHD) syndrome is shown in Figure 2-1.

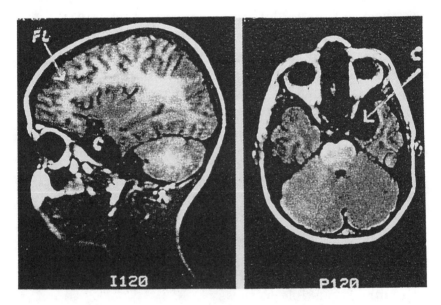

Figure 2-1. MRI showing temporal lobe arachnoid cyst (<---C) in a child presenting with ADHD. (FL = Frontal Lobe. C = Cyst)

Cysts of this type develop during pregnancy, and

are formed by an interruption of the normal development of the membranes surrounding the brain. They are sometimes associated with headache and seizures in addition to ADHD. The exact cause is usually undetermined, but an injury to the fetus is likely, stemming from trauma, bleeding, or virus infection. Treatment sometimes requires surgery to drain the cyst, but generally the symptoms can be controlled by other more conservative measures.

Measurements of various structures in the brain, using MRI quantitative techniques, have revealed changes in the development of the corpus callosum (the bridge connecting the right and left cerebral hemispheres), a decreased volume of the prefrontal cortex and basal ganglia on the right side of the brain, a smaller cerebellar vermis, and small cerebral volume.

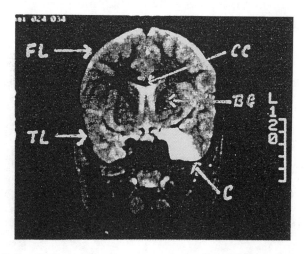

Figure 2-2. MRI coronal section through front of brain, showing corpus callosum (<--CC), basal ganglia (<--BG), frontal lobe (FL-->), and temporal lobe (TL-->). White areas are fluid in ventricles (center) and Cyst in left temporal lobe (lower right).

MRI measures of the right prefrontal cortex and basal ganglia correlate with response inhibition and task performance in ADHD children. Decreased cerebral volumes in some ADHD children may explain lower scores on IQ tests.

At the Western Psychiatric Institute, University of Pittsburgh, PA, MRI volumetric analyses in 26 children with ADHD compared to 26 normal controls showed correlations between task performance and prefrontal and caudate volume in the right hemisphere. Only right prefrontal measures correlated with performance of responses involving inhibition (Casey BJ et al, 1997).

At the National Institute of Mental Health, Bethesda, MD, quantitative MRI studies in 46 right-handed boys with ADHD and 47 matched healthy controls found a smaller cerebellar vermis, especially involving the posterior inferior lobules, in the ADHD group. A cerebello-thalamo-prefrontal circuit dysfunction is postulated in ADHD (Berquin PC et al, 1998).

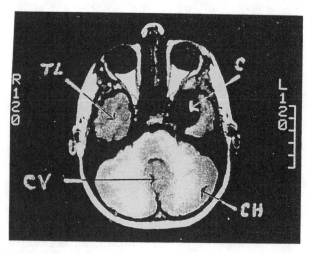

Figure 2-3. MRI showing cerebellar vermis (CV-->) and cerebellar hemisphere (<--CH). (TL = temporal lobe; C = cyst).

Localized cerebral hemisphere and cerebellar anomalies of development in ADHD are correlated with abnormal fronto-striatal-cerebellar function and sometimes with response to stimulant medication.

At the University of California, Irvine, volumetric MRI brain analyses in 15 male ADHD children compared to 15 normal controls showed smaller volumes of localized hemispheral structures. A smaller left basal ganglia (caudate nucleus specifically) was correlated with response to stimulant medication, whereas nonresponders had reversed caudate asymmetry (Filipek PA et al, 1997).

At the University of Barcelona, Spain, MRI measurements of the head of the caudate nucleus correlated with neuropsychological deficits and behavioral problems in 11 adolescents with ADHD. The ADHD group had a larger right caudate nucleus and a reversal of the normal L>R caudate asymmetry (Mataro M et al, 1997).

The different anatomical sites of injury or lesion in the brain, sometimes detected in children with ADHD, can account for the varying symptoms and complications of the syndrome. The role of the right hemisphere and especially the right frontal lobe in the neurological basis for ADHD is stressed by Voeller KKS (1990), my colleague, Charles Swisher, and others. The current research concerning structural cerebral anomalies in relation to ADHD has been reviewed in the author's series of "Progress in Pediatric Neurology I, II, & III" (Millichap JG, 1991, 1994, & 1997).

A frontal-motor cortex disconnection syndrome, or "lazy" frontal lobe, in ADHD is hypothesized on the basis of cerebral blood flow and EEG studies and MRI volumetric analyses (Niedermeyer E, Naidu SB, 1997). This concept is developed from the function of the frontal lobe as an inhibitor of excessive motor activity, children with ADHD having disinhibited motor activity. The calming effect of methylphenidate may stem from a stimulatory effect on the frontal lobe causing motor inhibition.

Q: Can head injury cause ADHD and learning disorders?

A: Head injury, even mild in degree, in young children warrants observation and follow-up for possible behavior and cognitive impairments.

Hyperactive behavior was directly correlated with the severity of head injury in a study of 95 children, aged 5 to 15 years, followed at the Johns Hopkins University, Baltimore (Greenspan AI, MacKenzie EJ, 1994). The risk of functional limitations following injury was increased in children with previous chronic health problems and those who sustained lower extremity injuries in addition to head injury.

Mild head injury, not sufficient to require admission to hospital for observation, can result in learning deficits and impairment of reading and school performance in young children.

Compared to a control group of preschool children with minor injury not involving the head, 78 head-injured preshoolers tested at one year after injury had visual perception problems and an increased incidence of dyslexia (Wrightson P et al, 1995). The development of visual skills necessary for reading were interrupted by the mild injury.

Math and spelling abilities were impaired in a 17-year-old boy who had sustained a right hemisphere injury in infancy. Investigations using a functional MRI at the University of Maryland, Baltimore, showed activation of the left hemisphere while the patient performed arithmetic calculations. Visuospatial skills normally subserved by the right hemisphere had been transferred to the left hemisphere after the injury, causing a "crowding effect" and disproportionate impairment of math and reading skills in comparison to language development (Levin HS et al, 1996).

At *Columbia University and New York State Psychiatric Institute,* low-birth-weight children, with neonatal cranial ultrasound abnormalities suggestive of white matter injury, were at increased risk for neuropsychiatric disorders, especially ADHD, by age 6 years (Whitaker AH et al, 1997).

Brain injury at an early age can lead to reorganization of the locations in the brain where language and cognitive function are represented.

Q: Can ADHD be inherited?

A: Parents will often admit that fathers and less often, the mothers were hyperactive or had a learning problem during childhood. Occasionally, they will deny any childhood behavior or attention problem, despite their inability to sit quietly during the consultation. A history of siblings and cousins who have been diagnosed with ADHD and who have had a favorable reponse to stimulant medications is not uncommon.

The clear distinction between the effects of nature and nurture in the cause of ADHD is difficult to prove, and both genetic and acquired factors are important. In some patients, the cause may be purely inherited, in others, mainly acquired and environmental, and in many, a combination of both. Several methods are employed by epidemiologists to demonstrate the role of genetic factors as compared to environmental influences. (Omen GS, 1973).

1) The prevalence of ADHD may vary in different geographic, ethnic, or racial populations.

In a study of 145 children diagnosed with ADHD at the Shaare Zedek Medical Center, Jerusalem, Israel, boys outnumbered girls by 3 to 1, 30% had siblings with learning disabilities compared to only 7% among control children without ADHD, and 34% were of North African descent, an ethnic background present in only 12% of the population of Jerusalem. A familial-genetic factor in this group of patients was expressed by the preponderance of males, the increased frequency of learning disabilities in siblings, and an ethnic-related propensity to ADHD (Gross-Tsur V et al, 1991).

2) First-degree relatives (parents, siblings, and children) of patients with ADHD have a higher risk than the general population of being affected.

Among 457 first degree relatives of children and adolescents referred to the Child Psychiatry Service, Massachusetts General Hospital, Boston, the risk of ADD, as well as antisocial and mood disorders, was significantly higher than among normal controls (Biederman J et al, 1990).

3) Identical, monozygotic (MZ) twins may be compared with fraternal, dizygotic (DZ) twins. If genetic factors are important, both MZ twins are affected (concordant), whereas concordance in DZ twins is lower and similar to that for ordinary siblings. DZ twins must be of the same sex in studies of ADHD, since there is a male preponderance. The extent to which MZ twins may be discordant (ie only one affected) is an indication of the influence of environmental factors in the cause of ADHD.

An evaluation of 10 pairs of twins, at least one having the hyperactive syndrome, showed that all four pairs of MZ twins were concordant, whereas only one of six DZ pairs was concordant. The MZ twins were all boys. (Lopez RE, 1965). This study supports a genetic basis for ADHD.

The Minnesota Twin Family Study, involving 576 twin boys, aged 11 and 12, and analyses of teacher and maternal reports, confirmed the importance of genetic factors in the mediation of both inattention and hyperactivity-impulsivity subtypes of ADHD. Environmental factors had lesser contributions to the etiology of ADHD (Sherman DK et al, 1997).

At the UCLA School of Medicine, Los Angeles, CA, twin studies using interview assessment of ADHD showed 79% concordance in 37 monozygotic twins compared to 32% in 37 same sex dizygotic twins. ADHD is a familial disorder, with frequency 5 to 6-fold greater among first degree relatives than in the general population. Relatives of ADHD probands have increased rates of comorbid conditions, especially oppositional and conduct disorders, anxiety, mood disorders, and learning disabilities. Adoption studies support both a genetic basis for ADHD and environmental factors (Smalley SL, 1997).

4) Comparison of MZ twins reared together versus MZ twins reared apart, in foster homes, allows epidemiologists to distinguish the influence of genetic from environmental factors within a family. Also, the incidence of ADHD in the biological vs the adoptive relatives or half-sibs can be determined.

In a study of full sibs and half-sibs of 14 children with minimal brain dysfunction (ADHD), all reared in foster homes, 50% of the full sibs vs 14% of the half-sibs had hyperactive behavior and attention deficits. (Safer DJ, 1969). These findings were more in favor of genetic than environmental influences in the cause of ADHD, although the study was flawed by a higher incidence of prematurity and neonatal difficulties among the full sibs, environmental factors known to cause ADHD.

These methods may point to the role of genetic factors in the cause of a disorder, but a specific metabolic or enzyme marker must be discovered in order to prove such an inherited predisposition. Well controlled studies of twins and adoptive environments are limited, and a metabolic marker for ADHD has not been uncovered. The evidence for environmental and acquired factors, although often presumptive, is perhaps stronger than the genetic data in the search for causes of ADHD.

In one large twin study, involving almost 2000 families recruited from the Australian MRC Twin Registry, and reported from the Prince of Wales Hospital, Randwick, NSW, ADHD is viewed as a continuum and not a discrete medical syndrome. ADHD is explained as an inherited trait with liability and expression throughout the population, a deviance from an acceptable norm, and not restricted to an arbitrary number of symptoms or DSM diagnostic criteria. The need for treatment including medication is relative, and dependent on multiple factors (Levy F et al, 1997).

Q: What is the frequency of learning disability and ADHD with neurofibromatosis?

A: Neurofibromatosis (von Recklinghausen's disease) is an inherited disease characterized by multiple tumors on the peripheral nerves and sometimes within the skull, and pigmentation areas in the skin, as well as lesions affecting the heart, bones and other organs. The disease has a frequency of 1 in 3000 and is transmitted as a dominant trait with many incomplete or abortive forms. About 10% of patients are mentally retarded, but 40% have hyperactivity with ADD and learning disorders.

Children with neurofibromatosis who are academic underachievers fall into one of three groups, psychologically. Approximately 40% have normal IQs, 50% have general learning disabilities, and 14% have visuospatial and motor coordination problems (Brewer VR et al, 1997). Cognitive impairments appear to correlate with the number and location of MRI brain abnormalities, especially hyperintense signals known as "unidentified bright objects" (UBOs) (Denckla MB et al, 1996; Moore BD et al, 1996).

Q: What is the role of an adverse home and school environment?

A: Adverse home circumstances and overcrowded classrooms may certainly contribute to and exacerbate hyperactivity and inattentiveness in a child with ADHD. However, these factors alone are rarely the explanation, and intrinsic genetic or acquired causes must always be investigated.

The influence of parents with psychiatric illness on the functioning of children with ADHD and normal conrol children was studied at the Pediatric Psychopharmacology Unit in Psychiatry, Massachusetts General Hospital, Boston, MA. The frequency of adverse family environments, including chronic family conflict, poor family union, and mothers with psychiatric problems, was greater among 140 ADHD compared to 120 normal children. (Biederman J et al, 1995).

Early recognition of these environmental factors should lead to prompt intervention and improved outcome.

In a study of psychiatric disorders in families of children with ADHD, at the Department of Pediatrics, Wyler and La Rabida Children's Hospitals, University of Chicago, alcoholism, drug abuse, depression, learning disabilities, and/or ADHD were more common among parents of ADHD than control children (with Down syndrome). (Roizen NJ et al, 1996).

Children with a family history of psychiatric disorders should be screened for ADHD.

Q: Are adopted children more susceptible?

A: In a previous analysis of the author's patients, the incidence of adoption among children with the hyperactive syndrome was 12% and more than three times the national incidence of adoption in that year (Millichap JG, 1975). A 17% rate of adoption was reported in another study of ADD children, 8 times that found in a normal control group or in the general population (Deutsch et al, 1982). Behavioral and psychiatric problems are not increased in the foster families of hyperactive adoptive children, according to another study. (Morrison J, Stewart M, 1973).

Although it is generally believed that behavior problems are more prevalent among adopted children, the occurrence of adverse psychological environments in foster or adoptive placements must not be assumed. An increased likelihood of insults to the fetus or newborn baby during unwanted pregnancies and births and possible genetic anomalies are more plausible explanations. In the author's ADD clinic at Children's Memorial Hospital, Chicago, cocaine exposure during pregnancy and birth is frequently reported by adoptive parents of foster children but is only rarely admitted by a biological parent.

*Q: What is the evidence for a biochemical
basis for ADHD?*

A: Evidence is accumulating that changes in the
brain chemistry - the catecholamine *neurotransmitters*
(dopamine, norepinephrine, and serotonin) - might
account for hyperactivity, inattentiveness and other
symptoms of ADHD. The central nervous system
stimulants, dextroamphetamine and methylphenidate
(Ritalin®), benefit ADHD by increasing catecholamine
concentrations in the brain. Catecholamine metabolism
and levels of norepinephrine are related to arousal,
attention span and motor activity.

The biochemical studies in children with ADHD are
experimental. Measurements of metabolites, or
breakdown products, of dopamine and norepinephrine
in the urine or of enzymes in the blood are not of
practical significance in the diagnosis and treatment of
ADHD, but they increase our understanding of the
neurobiology of ADHD (Zametkin AJ, Rapoport JL, 1987).

*Q: Can low blood sugar (hypoglycemia)
cause ADHD and learning disorders?*

A: Hypoglycemia in a newborn infant, if
unrecognized and untreated, can cause convulsions and
brain damage that later may result in mental
retardation or learning disorders and ADHD. Transient
hypoglycemia may occur in infants with birth anoxia
or other forms of perinatal stress, or in neonates born
to mothers with diabetes or toxemia.

Early onset childhood diabetes, before age 5 years, is often complicated by episodes of severe hypoglycemia that result in mild cognitive dysfunction, whereas late-onset diabetes, after age 5 years, and occasional episodes of severe hypoglycemia have no effect on cognitive function, according to a study in 28 diabetic children at the Trondheim University Hospital, Norway (Bjorgaas M et al, 1997).

Transient reactive hypoglycemia, following a diet of high sugar content, may be associated with behavioral symptoms seen with ADHD. A rapid rise in blood glucose can result in a heightened insulin secretion, with resultant hypoglycemic symptoms.

Q: Do sugar and other dietary factors play a role in the cause of ADHD?

A: Parents frequently note a worsening of hyperactivity and distractibility after the child with ADHD has eaten a high carbohydrate meal or a lot of candy. While the majority of scientifically controlled studies have failed to demonstrate a significant adverse effect, isolated reports tend to support the parents' observations.

In a study at Yale University School of Medicine, New Haven, CT, a fall in blood glucose at 3 to 5 hours after a glucose drink was accompanied by symptoms of hypoglycemia (shakiness, sweating, weakness, fast pulse) in children but not in adults. The reactive lowering of the blood glucose had stimulated a rise in plasma epinephrine, twice as high in children as in adults, sufficient to induce the symptoms of hypoglycemia. A measure of cognitive function, using evoked potentials, was significantly reduced when blood glucose was lowered below 75 mg/dl in children, but was preserved in adults until the level fell to 54 mg/dl (Jones TW et al, 1995).

Children appear to be more vulnerable to the effects of hypoglycemia on cognitive function than are adults. A diagnosis of excess sugar ingestion and reactive hypoglycemia as a cause of ADHD may be entertained when the child also suffers from more characteristic symptoms, including nervousness, tremor, sweating, dizziness, or palpitations.

At the Child Psychiatry Branch and Laboratory of Developmental Psychology, NIMH, Bethesda, MD, the effects of glucose, sucrose, saccharin, and aspartame on aggression and motor activity in 30 boys, ages 2 to 6 years, were compared. Eighteen boys were classed as "sugar responders" on parent questionnaires and 12 were "non-responders." Single dose challenges with sugar or sweetener, in a randomized, double-blind design, produced no significant differences in aggression or activity levels, as measured by teacher and parent ratings. The base-line duration of aggression in the alleged sugar responders correlated with the daily total sugar consumption, but acute sugar loading did not increase aggression or activity in preschool children (Krnesi MJP et al, 1987).

At the Schneider Children's Hospital, New York, the effect of a sucrose challenge on aggressive behavior and attention in a sample of hyperactive boys with ADD and age-matched control subjects was studied (Wender EH, Solanto MV, 1991). Aggression was not modified, but inattention measured by a continuous performance task was increased following sugar ingestion in the ADHD group. Conners CK at the National Children's Hospital, Washington, DC, reports that behavioral effects of sugar in children with ADHD may be demonstrated if the sucrose challenge follows a high carbohydrate breakfast. The effects are reversed or blocked if the child has a protein meal before or with the ingestion of sugar (Yehuda S, 1987)

An analysis of 16 published studies on the effects of sucrose on behavior and cognition of children with ADHD, conducted at Vanderbilt University, Nashville, TN, failed to demonstrate a significant adverse effect in the group as a whole, but a small effect in some sets of ADHD children could not be ruled out. (Wolraich ML et al, 1995). Aspartame (Nutrasweet®) used as a control in these studies was considered to have no adverse effect on behavior or cognition (Shaywitz BA et al, 1994), but further investigation of the safety of aspartame may be indicated. Some authorities have demonstrated an exacerbation of EEG seizure discharges and of migraine headaches following aspartame ingestion.

Q: Is there any significance to the Feingold theory of food additives as a cause of ADHD?

A: Controlled studies of the additive-free, Feingold diet have failed to demonstrate a significant benefit in children with ADHD, except in an occasional pre-school child. However, some parents still believe that their children are reactive to foods containing artificial coloring, flavoring agents and preservatives. They avoid apples, luncheon meats, sausage, hot dogs, gum, candies, cake mixes, oleomargarine, and ice cream. Flavored cold drinks, soda pop, and medicines containing aspirin are also excluded from the Feingold diet (1975).

The evidence for and against the Feingold theory is reviewed in Chapter 10. Scientific panels, established to study the efficacy of the diet and sponsored by the FDA, criticized the treatment and theory for lack of controls and statistical validity. Numerous studies of the effects of food additives on behavior followed, including additive-containing challenges. Small subgroups of younger children were found to react adversely to color additives in short-term trials, but the overwhelming benefits claimed by Dr Feingold were not substantiated (National Institutes of Health Consensus Panel, 1982).

The proof of food additive toxicity and relation to hyperactive behavior is difficult to determine. Questionnaires completed by parents, teachers, and psychologists may be biased, for or against, and may not address behavioral symptoms susceptible to the additive-free diet. Interest in the Feingold hypothesis and dietary treatment of ADHD has waned in the United States but waxes in Europe and Australia, where research continues on the use of elimination and hypoallergenic diets for the treatment of a variety of childhood neurobehavioral disorders.

Irritability, restlessness, and sleep disturbance rather than attention deficit were the behavioral patterns associated with the ingestion of azo dye food colorings (tartrazine and carmoisine) in a small, double-blind controlled study at the Royal Children's Hospital, Victoria, Australia (Rowe KS, 1988). The author concluded that behavioral rating questionnaires not including sleep habits may fail to identify specific reactors to food additives.

Q: What is the role of food allergy in ADHD?

A: Food allergy is proposed as a possible factor in the cause of ADHD. Chocolate, cow milk, egg, citrus, wheat, nuts and cheese have triggered hyperactive behavior in some susceptible patients, and a hypoallergenic, elimination diet has been used occasionally in practice (Millichap JG, 1986). A hyposensitization treatment with intradermal injections of food allergens (EPD) in 40 children with ADHD was conducted at the Universitatskinderklinik, Munchen, Germany, and the Great Ormond Street Hospital, London (Egger J et al, 1992). Of 20 children receiving the EPD injections, 16 no longer reacted toward hyperactivity-provoking foods, compared to 4 of 20 who received placebo shots. The role of food hypensitivity as a cause of ADHD is difficult to document in practice, the cooperation of neurologist, allergist, and dietician being essential. The hypoallergenic diet deserves further study.

Q: Is it necessary to examine thyroid function routinely in children with ADHD?

A: Routine testing for thyroid function in children with ADHD is probably unnecessary. A blood test for T3, T4, and TSH should be reserved for familial cases with short stature or a family history of thyroid disease. Impairments of cognition, attention, and behavior may occur with hypo- or hyper-thyroidism, and 70% of children having the rare disorder of generalized resistance to thyroid hormone (GRTH) also have been diagnosed with ADHD. However, of 53 boys with ADHD examined routinely for thyroid dysfunction at the Child Psychiatry Branch, NIMH, Bethesda, MD, none had GRTH based on T3, T4, and TSH values (Elia J, Rapoport JL et al, 1994). The authors conclude that GRTH is rare in

ADHD, and tests of thyroid function should be considered only in familial cases.

Optimal iodine intake is essential for normal thyroid function and the prevention of learning disabilities and academic underachievement. In the United States, iodine is present in the diet is adequate amounts but in underdeveloped countries, iodine deficiency is a common occurrence. Estimates find 200 million people affected by iodine deficiency diseases (IDD) and 800 million at risk worldwide, a total of 1 billion brains at risk of maldevelopment or malfunction!

The most serious complication of iodine deficiency diseases (IDD) is endemic cretinism, or congenital hypothyroidism, a cause of severe mental retardation. Milder forms of IDD can result in impaired cognitive function and learning disabilities in later childhood. IDD, a major international public health problem especially affecting underdeveloped countries, may be prevented by iodinized salt in the diet.

At the University of Groningen, The Netherlands, continuous performance tasks, measures of the ability to sustain attention, were used to study 48 children with early treated congenital hypothyroidism and 35 healthy controls. Impairments of sustained attention were correlated with low pre-treatment thyroid hormone levels but not with onset of treatment for hypothyroidism. Declines in sustained-attention task performance were related to cognitive, motor, and motivational deficits (Kooistra L et al, 1996).

At the Banjay Gandhi Postgraduate Institute of Medical Sciences, Lucknow, India, 100 boys with prolonged iodine deficiency, not suffering from cretinism and selected for their ability to read and write, were slow learners and had impaired motivation to achieve (Tiwari BD, Godpole MM et al, 1996).

Iodine deficiency not resulting in cretinism can cause learning disabilities and poor academic motivation.

Q: Can lead exposure cause ADHD?

A: Clinical reports suggest that lead-exposed children may be distractible and hyperactive, but few studies have examined the effects of lead on behavior using statistical controls. A characteristic "behavioral signature" associated with lead exposure has not been identified (Bellinger DC, 1995). Proof of cause and effect is often lacking, especially for conditions such as pervasive development disorder and speech articulation problems, sometimes claimed to be related to elevated blood lead levels.

Although the research is controversial, cognitive deficits have been correlated with blood lead levels of 10 mcg/dl or higher, and questions regarding risk of lead exposure at home, the school, or playground are important in children presenting with learning and behavior disorders. Preschool blood lead determinations are mandatory in some communities, but testing is appropriate in children diagnosed with ADHD and living in high risk environments.

At the Department of Community Medicine, University of Adelaide, Australia, a study of low level lead exposure and effects on intelligence, which began in 1979, has been followed into the primary school age range. In 494 children, aged 7 years, from a lead smelting community, the IQ was inversely related to antenatal and postnatal blood lead concentrations, even at 10 mcg/dl levels. An increase in blood lead from 10 to

30 mcg/dl caused deficits in verbal IQ and full scale IQ of 6 and 5 points, respectively (Baghurst PA et al, 1992).

Three longitudinal studies in different locations (Australia, Boston, Cincinnati) have demonstrated that lead-associated decreased intelligence is persistent across cultures, racial and ethnic groups, and social and economic classes. The finding is not limited to socially and economically disadvantaged children (Mahaffey KR, 1992).

Q: Are cocaine-exposed infants at risk for ADHD?

A: Cocaine-exposed infants require careful follow-up for early diagnosis and therapy of neurobehavioral complications. Foster children with ADHD attending my ADD clinic have a frequent history of prenatal cocaine exposure. A cause and effect is presumed but not proven.

At the University of Miami School of Medicine, FL, a study of 30 preterm cocaine-exposed infants compared to normal controls found smaller head circumference at birth, and a higher incidence of cerebral hemorrhage, restless sleep, agitated behavior, and tremulousness (Scafidi FA, Field TM et al, 1996).

These signs of abnormal brain development and excitation in cocaine-exposed infants were associated with higher levels of norepinephrine and dopamine in the urine, neurotransmitter chemicals important in the mechanism of ADHD. Hormonal changes, with higher cortisol levels and lower plasma insulin levels, were also reported in the cocaine-exposed newborns.

At the University of Florida, Gainesville, FL, cranial

ultrasound examinations of 134 cocaine-exposed compared to 132 control newborns found an increased incidence of brain cysts and enlarged ventricles, possibly related to cocaine effects on brain development (Behnke M et al, 1998).

At the Women and Infants Hospital, Brown University School of Medicine, Providence, RI, increased muscle tone and motor activity, jerky movements, startles, tremors, and back arching were observed in 20 infants with prenatal exposure to cocaine, alcohol, marijuana, and nicotine cigarettes (Napiorkowski B, Lester BM et al, 1996).

Signs of brain excitability were related only to cocaine and were not apparent in 17 infants exposed to alcohol, marijuana and nicotine without cocaine, nor in 20 drug-free infants.

At the Children's Hospital, Boston, MA, dose-related effects of cocaine on neurobehavior were demonstrated in exposed infants examined at 3 weeks of age. Heavily exposed infants showed impaired regulation of arousal and greater excitability than lightly or unexposed infants (Tronick EZ et al, 1996).

Effects of prenatal cocaine on behavior and development noted in infancy are likely precursors of ADHD in later childhood. A combination of cocaine exposure and poor nutrition is a cumulative risk factor for impaired infantile motor performance and later cognitive development in inner-city minority infants. Several papers have been published, all demonstrating adverse behavioral effects in neonates born to cocaine-addicted mothers. The details are reviewed in Progress in Pediatric Neurology III (Millichap JG, 1997).

Q: Does fetal exposure to alcohol, marijuana,

or cigarettes increase the risk of ADHD?

A: Behavioral problems are one of the characteristics of the "fetal alcohol syndrome" (FAS) that affects children born to mothers who consume alcohol during pregnancy. Alcohol use before a pregnancy has no adverse effect, but during pregnancy and breast feeding, alcohol may cause delay in an infant's development.

In addition to cognitive and behavior problems, the child with FAS has a small head, growth retardation, and facial peculiarities of development, or dysmorphisms. Premature infants of mothers who are high alcohol consumers are at increased risk for brain hemorrhage, according to a study of 349 infants at Michigan State University, East Lansing, MI (Holzman C et al, 1995).

In a study of 64 families with alcoholism at the Karolinska Institute, Stockholm, Sweden, children were retarded in development and had more behavioral problems than controls up to 4 years of age. Boys were more vulnerable than girls. Behavioral disorders were more pronounced when both parents were alcoholic (Nordberg L et al, 1994).

At Sahlgren University Hospital, Goteborg, Sweden, 26 children of mothers who abused alcohol during pregnancies were followed throughout childhood and were examined at 11 to 14 years of age for neuropsychiatric, psychological, and social problems. Of 24 seen at follow-up, 10 had ADHD, 2 had Asperger syndrome, and one had mild mental retardation and autistic spectrum disorder. The severity of the disorder was correlated with the degree of alcohol exposure in utero. Children whose mothers discontinued alcohol consumption by the 12th week of gestation developed normally and had no learning problems in school (Aronson M et al, 1997).

Biological, not psychosocial, factors are responsible for ADHD in children with fetal alcohol syndrome.

Maternal cigarette smoking has been linked to impairments of cognitive function and memory, academic under-achievement, and behavioral problems in children exposed during pregnancy (Drews CD et al, 1996). In a follow-up study of 6 year old children studied at Carleton University, Ottawa, Ontario, Canada, prenatal marijuana was associated with errors of omission in tasks of vigilance, reflecting a deficit in sustained attention (Fried PA et al, 1992).

Cigarette smoking, marijuana use, and alcohol excess during pregnancy may have adverse effects on the behavior and attention of the infant and child, but a definite causative role in ADHD has not been established.

Q: Are PCBs and other environmental toxins potential causes of ADHD?

A: Environmental contaminants of our food and water supplies include PCBs (polychlorinated biphenyls), PBBs (polybrominated biphenyls), nitrates, DDT, dioxin, mercury and lead. DDT and other pesticides, including dioxin, and PCBs have not been produced since the 1970s. Despite the ban on the manufacture of these chemicals, dangerous concentrations persist in the water of rivers and inland lakes.

PCBs were dumped years ago as waste products from electrical transformer, capacitor, and plasticizer factories. From the sediment at the bottom of harbors, hazardous waste residues pollute the water and are eaten by microscopic organisms and fish. From fish the chemicals are passed to birds and humans, causing various ailments including cancer and reproductive problems (Millichap JG, 1993, 1995). Man is the final consumer in the food chains, and he is exposed to the greatest concentrations of any environmental poison.

While regulatory control measures have substantially reduced the PCB contamination of animal feeds and food products by spillage, those subgroups of the population who regularly consume fish caught in lakes and streams are still at risk of poisoning. Surveys and analyses of fish from the Hudson River in New York State and from Lake Michigan showed significant levels of contamination with PCBs in excess of 5 ppm.

Studies designed to assess the health hazard of PCB exposure from Lake Michigan fish showed a correlation between the quantity of fish consumed and the concentration of PCB in blood and breast milk of participants in the studies. Those eating higher amounts of fish had significantly higher blood levels of PCB. Children born to women who routinely consumed Lake Michigan sportfish displayed poorer short-term memory function on both verbal and quantitative tests. The cognitive function was tested at 11 years of age in 212 children exposed prenatally to PCBs and examined at Wayne State University, Detroit, MI (Jacobson JL, Jacobson SW, 1996). Long-term intellectual impairment affected memory, attention, and reading ability, deficits frequently found in children with ADHD.

Developmental neurotoxicity of PCBs is reviewed in a publication from the Institute of Environmental Studies, University of Illinois at Urbana-Champaign, Illinois (Schantz SL, 1996). Studies included reports from Yusho, Japan; Yucheng,

Taiwan; Michigan; North Carolina; Oswego, NY; New Bedford, MA; on Inuit people in the Arctic regions of Quebec; and in Faroe Islanders. Methylmercury poisoning could be an additional contaminant in some studies.

Children born to mothers exposed to PCBs showed abnormalities in behavior and development, including higher activity levels, lower IQ scores, decreased birth weight and head circumference, deficits in memory at 4 years, and delays in psychomotor development. The public health implications of low-level PCB exposure was compared to that of lead exposure. The effect of PCB was either by direct injury to the brain in the prenatal period or secondary to effects on thyroid function.

At Odense University, Denmark, a study of 1022 children born 1986-1987 in the Faroe Islands to mothers who had consumed methylmercury-polluted pilot whale meat found deficits in language, attention, and memory at 7 years of age (Grandjean P et al, 1997).

Subtle alterations in neuropsychological functioning caused by exposure to these environmental toxins are proposed as potential causes for some cases of ADHD and learning disabilities.

Q: Could diet during infancy have a role in the cause of ADHD?

A: Diets during infancy have been studied in relation to adult diseases such as hypertension and heart attack. Researchers at Columbia University, New York, have studied the rate of weight gain and diet-dependent changes in biochemistry, physiology, and behavior of 142 preterm infants fed varied protein and energy intakes (de Klerk A et al, 1997).

Rapidly growing infants had increased heart rates,

respiratory rates, active sleep time, and decreased EEG frequencies compared to slow growing infants. Shifts in the balance of catecholamine and serotonergic neurotransmitters, similar to those reported with ADHD, were proposed as the cause of the changes in autonomic responses related to diet and rapid growth.

Nutrition and weight gain during infancy may be a factor in the etiology of ADHD.

REFERENCES

Aronson M et al. Attention deficits and autistic spectrum problems in children exposed to alcohol during gestation: a follow-up study. Dev Med Child Neurol 1997;39:583-587.

Baghurst PA et al. Environmental exposure to lead and children's intelligence at the age of seven years. N Engl J Med 1992;327:1279-1284.

Behnke M et al. Fetal cocaine exposure and brain abnormalities. J Pediatr 1998;132:291-294.

Bellinger DC. Interpreting the literature on lead and child development: The neglected role of the "experimental system." Neurotoxicol Teratol 1995;17:201-212.

Berquin PC et al. Cerebellum in attention-deficit hyperactivity disorder. A morphometric MRI study. Neurology 1998;50:1087-1093.

Biederman J et al. Family-genetic and psychosocial risk factors in DSM-III attention deficit disorder. J Am Acad Child Adolesc Psychiatry 1990;29:527-533.

Biederman J et al. Impact of adversity on functioning and comorbidity in children with attention-deficit hyperactivity disorder. J Am Acad Child Adolesc Psychiatry 1995;34:1495-1503.

Bjorgaas M et al. Cognitive function in type 1 diabetic children with and without episodes of severe hypoglycemia. Acta Pediatr 1997;86:148-153.

Brewer VR et al. Learning disability subtypes in children with neurofibromatosis. Jrnl of Learning Disabilities 1997;30:521-533.

Casey BJ et al. Implication of right frontostriatal circuitry in response inhibition and attention-deficit/hyperactivity disorder. J Am Acad Child Adolesc Psychiatry 1997;36:374-383.

de Klerk A et al. Diet and infant behavior. Acta Pediatr (Suppl 422) 1997;86:65-68.

DeLong GR, Heinz ER. The clinical syndrome of early-life bilateral hippocampal sclerosis. Ann Neurol 1997;42:11-17.

Denckla MB et al. Relationship between T2-weighted hyperintensities (unidentified bright objects) and lower IQs in children with neurofibromatosis-1. Am J Med Genet 1996;67:98-102.

Deutch C et al. Overrepresentation of adoptees in children with attention deficit disorder. Behav Genet 1982;12:231-237.

Drews CD et al. Maternal smoking is a preventable cause of mental retardation. Pediatrics 1996;97:547-553.

Egger J et al. Controlled trial of hyposensitization in children with food-induced hyperkinetic syndrome. Lancet 1992;339:1150-1153.

Elia J, Rapoport JL et al. Thyroid function and attention-deficit hyperactivity disorder. J Am Acad Child Adolesc Psychiatry 1994;33:169-172.

Feingold BF. Why Your Child is Hyperactive. New York. Randon House, 1975.

Filipek PA et al. Volumetric MRI analysis comparing subjects having attention-deficit hyperactivity disorder with normal controls. Neurology 1997;48:589-601.

Fried PA et al. A follow-up study of attentional behavior in 6-year-old children exposed prenatally to marijuana, cigarettes, and alcohol. Neurotoxicol Teratol 1992;14:299-311.

Grandjean P et al. Cognitive deficit in 7-year-old children with prenatal exposure to methylmercury. Neurotoxicol Teratol 1997;19:417-428.

Greenspan AI, MacKenzie EJ. Functional outcome after pediatric head injury. Pediatrics 1994;94:425-432.

Gross-Tsur V et al. Attention deficit disorder: association with familial-genetic factors. Ped Neurol 1991;7:258-261.

Holzman C et al. Perinatal brain injury in premature infants born to mothers using alcohol in pregnancy. Pediatrics 1995;95:66-73.

Jacobson JL, Jacobson SW. Intellectual impairment in children exposed to polychlorinated biphenyls in utero. N Engl J Med 1996;335:783-789.

Jones TW et al. Enhanced adrenomedullary response and increased susceptibility to neuroglycopenia: Mechanisms underlying the adverse effects of sugar ingestion in healthy children. J Pediatr 1995;126:171-177.

Kooistra L et al. Sustained attention problems in children with early treated congenital hypothyroidism. Acta Paediatr 1996;85:425-429

Krnesi MJP et al. Effects of sugar and aspartame on aggression and activity in children. Am J Psychiatry 1987;144:1487-1490.

Levy F et al. ADHD as a continuum, not a discrete entity. J Am Acad Child Adolesc Psychiatry 1997;36:737-744.

Lopez RE. Hyperactivity in twins. Can Psychiatr Assoc J 1965;10:421.

Mahaffey KR. Lead exposure and IQ in children. Editorial. N Engl J Med 1992;327:1308.

Mataro M et al. Magnetic resonance imaging measurement of the caudate nucleus in adolescents with attention-deficit hyperactivity disorder and its relationship with neuropsychological and behavioral measures. Arch Neurol 1997;54:963-968.

Millichap JG. The Hyperactive Child with Minimal Brain Dysfunction. Questions and Answers. Chicago, Year Book, 1975.

Millichap JG. Nutrition, Diet, and Your Child's Behavior. Springfield, Illinois, Charles C Thomas, 1986.

Millichap JG. Environmental Poisons in Our Food. Chicago, PNB Publishers, 1993.

Millichap JG. Is Our Water Safe to Drink? Chicago, PNB Publishers, 1995.

Millichap JG. Temporal lobe arachnoid cyst-attention deficit disorder syndrome. Neurology 1997;48:1435-1439.

Millichap JG. Ed. Progress in Pediatric Neurology I, II, & III. Chicago, PNB Publishers, 1991, 1994, & 1997.

Moore BD et al. Neuropsychological significance of areas of high signal intensity on brain MRIs of children with neurofibromatosis. Neurology 1996;46:1660-1668.

Morrison J, Stewart M. The psychiatric status of legal families of adopted hyperactive children. Arch Gen Psychiatry 1973;28:888-891.

Napiorkowski B, Lester BM et al. Effects of in utero substance exposure on infant neurobehavior. Pediatrics 1996;98:71-75.

Nordberg L et al. Familial alcoholism and neurobehavior in children. Acta Paediatr 1994;Suppl 404:14-18.

Omen GS. Genetic issues in the syndrome of minimal brain dysfunction. In: Walzer S, Wolff PH. (eds). Minimal Cerebral Dysfunction in Children. New York. Grune & Stratton. 1973.

Roizen NJ et al. Psychiatric and developmental disorders in families of children with ADHD. Arch Pediatr Adolesc Med 1996;150:203-208.

Safer DJ. The familial incidence of minimal brain dysfunction. Unpublished study. 1969. In: Wender PH. Minimal Brain Dysfunction in Children. New York, Wiley-Interscience, 1971.

Scafidi FA, Field TM et al. Cocaine-exposed preterm neonates show behavioral and hormonal differences. Pediatrics 1996;97:851-855.

Schantz SL. Developmental neurotoxicity of polychlorinated biphenyls (PCBs) in humans. Neurotoxicol and Teratology 1996;18:217-227.

Shaywitz BA et al. Aspartame, behavior, and cognitive function in children with attention deficit disorder. Pediatrics 1994;93:70-75.

Sherman DK et al. Attention-deficit hyperactivity disorder dimensions: a twin study of inattention and impulsivity-hyperactivity. J Am Acad Child Adolesc Psychiatry 1997;36:745-753.

Smalley SL. Behavioral genetics '97. Genetic influences in childhood-onset psychiatric disorders: autism and attention deficit/hyperactivity disorder. Am J Hum Genet 1997;60:1276-1282.

Tiwari BD, Godbole MM et al. Learning disabilities and poor motivation to achieve due to prolonged iodine deficiency. Am J Clin Nutr 1996;63:782-786.

Tronick EZ et al. Late dose-response effects of prenatal cocaine exposure on neurobehavioral performance. Pediatrics 1996;98:76-83.

Voeller KKS. The neurological basis of attention deficit hyperactivity disorder. Int Pediatr 1990;5:171-176.

Whitaker AH et al. Psychiatric outcomes in low-birth-weight

children at age 6 years: Relation to neonatal cranial ultrasound abnormalities. Arch Gen Psychiatry 1997;54:847-856.

Wrightson P et al. Mild head injury in preschool children: Evidence that it can be associated with a persisting cognitive defect. J Neurol Neurosurg Psychiatry 1995;59:375-380.

Yehuda S. Brain biochemistry and behavior. Nutrition Reviews/Supplement May 1986;44:1-250.

Yehuda S. Effects of dietary nutrients and deficiencies on brain biochemistry and behavior. Intern J Neuroscience 1987;35:21-36.

Zametkin AJ, Rapoport JL. Neurobiology of attention deficit disorder with hyperactivity: Where have we come in 50 years? J Am Acad Child & Adolesc Psychiatry 1987;26:676-686.

CHAPTER **3**

SYMPTOMS AND SIGNS OF ADHD

The symptoms of ADHD are outlined in the DSM-IV diagnostic criteria in two main subtypes or groups: 1) symptoms of inattentiveness, and 2) hyperactivity-impulsivity. Signs of brain dysfunction and associated perceptual and learning disabilities are omitted from the current definition, as outlined by the American Psychiatric Association. The recognition of both symptoms and signs of ADHD is considered important by neurologists, however, particularly in terms of defining the cause and treatment.

ADHD as defined by the DSM-IV rarely occurs alone. Certain neuropsychiatric disorders frequently complicate the diagnosis of ADHD, and often modify the treatment. Many of these disorders are neurological, including headache, seizures, tics or Tourette syndrome, and speech and language and motor coordination problems. Others are psychiatric or neuropsychological in nature, principally oppositional defiance disorder (ODD), and conduct disorder (CD).

The differential diagnosis, or conditions that may present with some of the symptoms of ADHD, includes bipolar disorders (depression, dysthymia), pervasive developmental disorders (autism, Asperger's syndrome), personality disorders (obsessive compulsive disorder (OCD)), and mental retardation syndromes. The physician or psychologist who treats children with ADHD needs to be familiar with all associated disorders that may require investigation and specialized methods of management.

Q: When is "inattentiveness" an "attention deficit disorder?"

A: Most children have periods of "day dreaming" in school when attention wanders transiently, but not sufficiently to impair learning. Inattentiveness becomes an attention deficit disorder (ADD) when the child is unable to sustain attention and is frequently distracted by outside stimuli. In order to attend, the child must ignore or tune out irrelevant distracting stimuli. The child with ADD fails to inhibit the background "noise" in the classroom environment (Rosenberger PB, 1991). Symptoms of ADD also include a listening problem, forgetfulness, weakness in organization, and inability to complete a task.

If the inattentiveness is episodic and the child appears confused, the possibility of absence or partial complex seizures is considered and an electroencephalogram (EEG) is recommended. The distinction between a sustained inattentiveness, characteristic of ADD, and seizures is important in determining the medical management. The stimulant medication frequently prescribed for ADD may worsen the episodes of inattention related to a seizure disorder.

Q: How is attention measured?

A: Measures of attention involve the direct observation of the child or the indirect questioning of parents and teachers. Direct measures of attention are of three types: 1) By recording the alpha rhythm on the electroencephalogram (EEG) and by evoked potentials (EP); 2) Tests of reaction time, continuous performance tests, paired associated learning, and tests of memorization; and 3) Psychometric tests such as the WISC, Stanford-Binet, Detroit, and Reading achievement. Measures 1 and 2 are mainly relevant in research and have little application in clinical practice.

The EEG alpha activity (8-13 Hz) reflects a state of relaxation and inattention to the environment, and the fast beta activity (14-25 Hz) is activated by emotional and cognitive processes (Ray W, Cole H, 1985).

Computerized quantitative analysis of the EEG, performed at the University of Tennessee, Knoxville, TN in 25 boys with ADHD compared to 27 matched controls, showed a decrease in beta and an increase in theta (4-7 Hz) activity. These differences were enhanced in ADHD subjects during reading and drawing tasks, especially in frontal areas of the head (Mann CA, 1992). Increases in the latency of the P300 wave, an evoked response generated by attention, correlates with cognitive impairment (Finley W et al, 1985).

Reaction time has been used to demonstrate attentiveness and cognitive improvement after stimulant therapy (Sprague R et al, 1970). Divided attention to multiple stimuli has been monitored by reinforcement, using operant conditioning to study visual inattention in subjects with parietal lobe damage (Rosenberger P, 1974). The continuous performance test (CPT), using errors of commission or omission as measures of inattention to change of stimuli and impulsivity, is complex and allows some children to compensate for an AD (Trommer BL et al, 1988). The paired associate learning (PAL) test, using the coding or digit symbol subtest of the WISC, is sensitive to the inattention and distractibility of the learning-disabled child with ADHD (Kinsbourne M, Conners C, 1990), as are standard memory tests..

Learning requires attention, and psychometric measures of cognitive function are sensitive to inattention. Analysis of the WISC intelligence subtests - arithmetic, digit span, and coding - demonstrates relatively low scores in hyperactive children, a reflection of the adverse effects of inattention and distractibility on learning. Attention deficit interferes with the performance of several additional tests of intelligence and short-term memory: the Stroop Color and Word Test, the Stanford-Binet Intelligence Scale, the Detroit Test of Learning Aptitudes, and the MacGinitie Reading Test. Neuropsychological testing is an essential part of the investigation of the child with ADHD.

The Conners questionnaire (1969) is the earliest and most widely used measure of attention deficit in children with ADHD. Parent and teacher questionnaires are either short or long. They usually use a 4-point rating system, and they distinguish the factors of hyperactivity, inattention, impulsivity, and peer interaction.

Q: When is hyperactivity abnormal?

A: Children normally have an excessive degree of motor restlessness at times, particularly in emotionally charged environments. Hyperactive behavior is abnormal when accompanied by short attention span and distractibility, and when it is purposeless, inappropriate and undirected toward a specific, meaningful goal. The inability to focus and perform structured tasks is the hallmark of the hyperactive school-age child. The quality and direction of the hyperactivity are abnormal, not necessarily the total daily activity. Hyperactivity is frequently accompanied by impulsivity, a tendency to interrupt others and inability to wait in line.

The child with ADHD is often restless in infancy. As a toddler, he "is into everything," and has to be watched constantly for his own protection and that of household breakables. In later childhood, he is constantly fidgeting, always "on the go," and is unable to sit still at the dinner table. At school, the teacher also reports an inability to sit still, he gets up and walks around in the classroom, he talks excessively, interrupts, and tends to distract and disturb others. The motor hyperactivity is often accompanied by "verbal hyperactivity," and sometimes a flight of ideas, without focus on the topic of conversation.

In anatomical studies of the origin of hyperactivity, two types are distinguished: 1) *overreactivity* caused by frontal lobe injury and a response to external environmental stimulation; and 2) *essential overactivity* caused by striatal lesions and a release of motor activity normally inhibited by frontal-striatal connections in the brain (Magoun HW, 1963; Millichap JG, 1997). We may infer that some children with ADHD are overreactive only when stimulated by a noisy environment, whereas others exhibit a constant uninhibited motor activity unrelated to the environment. The hyperactivity may appear normal in the playground but abnormal and inappropriate in the classroom.

Q: What devices are available to measure motor activity?

A: Several methods have been used experimentally to measure the degree of motor activity. These include the pedometer, to quantify gross locomotor activity; a stabilimetric cushion, to record the degree of wiggling or fidgeting; and a grid-marked floor, which permits assessment of the time spent in one activity or the degree of mobility from one location in a room to another. The author has used a device called an "actometer," an automatically winding calendar wrist watch with the pendulum connected directly to the hands, so that movements of either arms or legs may be recorded in minutes and hours. The actometer was used to demonstrate the beneficial effects of methylphenidate in one of the first controlled studies of medications for the treatment of ADHD, conducted at Children's Memorial Hospital, Northwestern University, Chicago, IL (Millichap JG et al, 1968).

More recently, an infrared video and motion analysis system was used at the Department of Psychiatry, Harvard Medical School, Boston, to record movement patterns of 18 boys with ADHD and 11 normal controls during a continuous performance task (CPT) (Teicher MH et al, 1996). Compared to controls, subjects with ADHD moved their extremities and head more than twice as often, and they covered a 3-fold greater distance and a 4-fold greater area. Whole body movements were also 3 to 4 times more frequent. Responses on the CPT were slower and more variable. The movement patterns of ADHD children correlated with the teacher ratings of hyperactivity and inattention. The authors are also experimenting with a device similar to the "actometer," and called an "actigraph," a wristwatch-sized recorder worn on a belt.

These objective measures of motor activity are of value in experimental situations, particularly in trials of new medical treatments. They may also be indicated for the confirmation of diagnosis of overactivity when parent and teacher impressions are in disagreement. From a practical standpoint in the everyday management of the child with ADHD they are of limited value.

Q: What are so-called "soft" neurologic signs?

A: Mild or subtle neurologic abnormalities are sometimes referred to as "soft" signs. Many children with ADHD are described as clumsy or uncoordinated. They may be poor at sports, especially basketball and activities requiring a quick reaction and facile movements. A neurologist will identify signs of immaturity or delayed development of the nervous system. Sometimes, the clumsiness and soft signs will persist into adult life. Unlike cerebral palsy, the incoordination of movement is not associated with obvious muscle weakness or spasticity. Movements (synkinetic or mirror) that are normally inhibited by five years of age persist into older age groups, and coordination abilities (hopping and tandem gait) usually accomplished by five years are delayed.

Motor impersistence is a characteristic neurologic soft sign of ADHD. The term was first coined to describe the difficulty in maintaining a motor behavior experienced by brain injured adults, even though they had no problem in initiating or performing the movements. The injury was located in the right hemisphere of the brain, especially the frontal lobe, an area often involved in ADHD. Motor impersistence is manifested by an inability to maintain movements such as the following on request: "close your eyes," "look at my nose or finger," "put out your tongue," or " hold your arms outstretched."

Response inhibition deficit. In addition to motor impersistence, the child with ADHD demonstrates an inability to inhibit responses. A child will be unable to look away from a stimulus when requested. When asked to hold out the arms and stand still, he will frequently initiate other movements such as walking. The teacher will complain, "he can't keep his hands to himself." If he sees a pencil or a pair of scissors, he is unable to look at the object without putting it to its intended use. The neurologist calls this sign "utilization behavior." These deficits in response inhibition are a reflection of inattentiveness, the tendency to respond to distracting stimuli, and of impulsivity (Voeller KKS, 1990).

Dyspraxia or *apraxia* is another soft neurologic sign commonly recognized in association with ADHD. Dyspraxia is a loss of dexterity in purposeful movements, as in hopping, tandem walking, or the use of scissors, despite normal muscle strength. The term dyspraxia is also applied to an inability to protrude the tongue on command, yet the movement is carried out involuntarily. A delay in speech may be a form of apraxia. A constructional apraxia is an inability to build blocks or copy simple designs. Dyspraxias are caused by dysfunction or damage to the frontal lobes of the brain.

Dysdiadochokinesia is a clumsy neurological term for clumsiness in the performance of rapidly alternating movements (pronation and supination) of the forearms. Children aged 5 to 7 years should be able to imitate the examiner's movements without mirroring the movement in the opposite forearm. Involuntary mirror movements are referred to as *synkinesia,* and are a common sign of minimal brain dysfunction in ADHD. When the child is older he is usually able to inhibit these mirror movements.

Ataxia and incoordination, also described as clumsiness, may represent an immaturity or damage to the cerebellum and its connections. An attempt to walk a straight line is performed unsteadily, and finger-to-nose movements of the upper limbs bring out a tremor.

Choreiform movements are involuntary jerky movements, usually demonstrated by asking the child to stretch out his arms. They were described in children with minimal brain dysfunction by Prechtl (1962). In my experience, choreiform movements are not a common or characteristic sign of ADHD.

Graphanesthesia is a sensory impairment, an

inability to recognize numerals traced on the skin of the palms or the back. It is caused by dysfunction of the parietal lobes of the brain.

Other abnormal neurologic signs include a tendency to walk on the toes due to tight heel cords or contractures of the Achilles tendons, and Babinski signs, an extension of the great toe and fanning of the second to the fifth toes when the plantar surface of the foot is stroked with a blunt object. These signs are not included under the term "soft" neurologic abnormalities, since they commonly persist and may be evidence of permanent dysfunction of the pyramidal tracts and cerebrospinal motor system.

These neurological signs were of predictive value for learning disabilities in preschool children, aged 3 to 5 years, followed at the Wyler Children's Hospital, University of Chicago, IL (Huttenlocher PR et al, 1990). A poor neurologic test score at age five correlated with a lower Full-scale IQ at age seven, and neurologic soft signs accurately identified nearly all the children who needed special educational help.

Abnormal neurologic signs identical to those included in the above test battery have previously been correlated with hyperactive behavior, ADHD, and a beneficial response to stimulant medication (Millichap JG, 1974).

A careful examination and recording of neurologic abnormalities helps in our understanding of the causes and anatomical lesions in the brain that may explain the mechanism of ADHD. The need for special diagnostic laboratory investigations such as EEG and MRI is determined by the neurological history and findings.

REFERENCES

Conners C. A teacher rating scale for use in drug studies with children. Am J Psychiatry 1969;126:152-156.

Finley W et al. Long-latency event-related potentials in the evaluation of cognitive function in children. Neurology 1985;35:323-327.

Kinsbourne M, Conners C. eds. Diagnosis and Treatment of Attention Deficit Disorders. Munich, MMW Press, 1990.

Magoun HW. The Waking Brain, 2nd ed, Springfield, IL, Charles C Thomas, 1963.

Mann CA. Quantitative analysis of EEG in boys with attention-deficit-hyperactivity disorder: Controlled study with clinical implications. Pediatr Neurol 1992;8:30-36.

Millichap JG et al. Hyperactive behavior and learning disorders: Battery of neuropsychological tests in controlled trial of methylphenidate. Am J Dis Child 1968;116:237-244.

Millichap JG. Methylphenidate in hyperkinetic behavior: Relation of response to degree of activity and brain damage. In: Conners CK, ed, Clinical Use of Stimulant Drugs in Children. Amsterdam, Excerpta Medica 1974.

Prechtl HFR, Stemmer C. The choreiform syndrome in children. Dev Med Child Neurol 1962;4:119.

Ray W, Cole H. EEG alpha activity reflects attentional demands and beta activity reflects emotional and cognitive processes. Science 1985;228:750-752.

Rosenberger PB. Discriminative aspects of visual hemi-inattention. Neurology 1974;24:18-23.

Rosenberger PB. Attention deficit. Pediatr Neurol 1991;7:397-405.

Sprague R et al. Methylphenidate and thioridiazine: Learning, reaction time, activity, and classroom behavior in disturbed children. Am J Orthopsychiatry 1970;40:615-

628.

Teicher MH et al. Objective measurement of hyperactivity and attentional problems in ADHD. J Am Acad Child Adolesc Psychiatry 1996;35:334-342.

Trommer BL et al. Pitfalls in the use of a continuous performance test as a diagnostic tool in attention deficit disorder. J Dev Behav Pediatr 1988;9:339-346.

Voeller KKS. The neurological basis of attention deficit hyperactivity disorder. Int Pediatr 1990;5:171-176.

CHAPTER 4

DIAGNOSIS AND SPECIAL TESTS

The diagnosis of ADHD is determined by an evaluation of reports from parents and teachers and by observation and examination of the child in the office of the physician or psychologist. The parents and teachers will provide completed questionnaires that rate attention, behavior, impulsivity, and social skills. Since the symptoms of ADHD are especially troublesome when the child enters school, the teacher is often the first to draw attention to the problem and advise the parents to consult a pediatric neurologist.

The visit to the physician will include questions about the pregnancy, birth, early development and family history. The reports of achievements and difficulties in preschool, kindergarten and grade school will be evaluated. The history taking is followed by a neurologic examination and a review of any tests previously ordered by the pediatrician, family practitioner, or psychologist. The response to any previous treatments will be discussed.

If the physician agrees with the diagnosis of ADHD he will attempt to determine the cause and the need for special tests. The indications for EEG, MRI, blood analyses, chromosome studies, and neuropsychological evaluation will be reviewed. The pros and cons of stimulant or other types of medication will be determined after all criteria for the diagnosis of ADHD and complicating medical conditions have been met.

Q: What questions will the neurologist ask?

A: A parent should be prepared to answer the following questions at a pediatric neurology consultation:

• What are your main concerns and when did the symptoms begin? Are the hyperactivity and/or inattentiveness present both in the home and at school?

• What is your child's grade placement, the number of pupils in the class, the type of school, and is the education bilingual? Were any grades repeated?

• Has the teacher suggested the consultation and did you bring a written report or completed questionnaire regarding behavior, attention, and achievement?

• Was mother well during the pregnancy or did she suffer from infection, diabetes, or trauma, or use alcohol, tobacco or drugs? Does she take thyroid hormone?

• Was the birth normal or complicated? What was the birth weight? Was the birth premature? What were the Apgar scores or vital signs at birth? Did the baby breathe normally or need resuscitation? Did jaundice develop and require treatment? How long was the baby in the hospital?

• What were the milestones of early development? Did the child walk by 14 months, talk in short phrases by 2 years, pedal a tricycle by 3 years, and know colors by 5 years?

• Is there any history of seizures, fever convulsions, episodic daydreaming or confused appearance, headaches, sleep disorders, enuresis, head trauma, tics, ear infections, asthma, or other illness requiring chronic medication?

• Have vision and hearing been checked? Has the blood lead level been tested by the pediatrician?

• Does your child exhibit any other behavioral problems that sometimes complicate ADHD, such as oppositional defiance or conduct disorder.

• Do other members of the family have a history of ADHD or related neuropsychiatric problems? Are there siblings, and what are their ages and academic placements and achievements? What is the health and occupation of the parents? Is the family environment supportive or divided?

Q: What is involved in a pediatric neurology examination?

A: The neurologic examination is largely a fun-filled experience for the child. No "shots" should be expected, unlike the usual visit to a pediatrician's office. The child should be reassured that the examination is painless?

The demeanor of the child is observed. Is he or she happy and smiling or sad and impassive, cooperative or negative, quick to understand and follow simple directions or slow in reaction time, and does he relate well or poorly to the examiner, his parents, and siblings in the office setting? Does he have career goals or does he lack motivation? Most children, even as young as 5 years of age, will have an idea of what they would like to do as adults. In the younger child, the most common preference is a policeman or fireman, rarely a doctor or lawyer, independent of the socioeconomic status.

Tests of cranial nerve function include a clinical assessment of vision and hearing, an examination of the optic nerve and retina of the eye (funduscopic exam), eye, facial and tongue movements, and speech and language fluency.

The motor system examination involves the gait, balance, coordination, alternating movements of the forearms, involuntary movements such as tics and tremors, reflexes, muscle power and tone, and handedness. The sensory system includes touch localization and the ability to recognize numerals traced on the skin.

The general physical examination includes measurements of head circumference, height and weight, heart sounds and blood pressure, birth marks and congenital developmental anomalies or dysmorphisms. Finally, the neurologist may ask the child to copy simple shapes, draw a person, read a paragraph, and write his name and a sentence about the weather, although the interpretation of these tests is generally the province of the psychologist.

Q: What are the indications for an EEG?

A: The neurologist may consider the need for an EEG in the following circumstances:

• A history of seizures, febrile convulsions, or frequent "daydreaming" and lapses of memory.
• Recurrent headaches, especially when complicated by vomiting or the need to lie down.
• A history of head trauma, encephalitis or meningitis preceding the onset of ADHD.
• In patients with a past history or family history of epilepsy, as a precursor to treatment with buproprion, imipramine, or methylphenidate, drugs known to precipitate seizures in susceptible patients.

Q: What are the indications for an MRI or CT scan in a child with ADHD?

A: An imaging study of the head, MRI or CT scan, is indicated for the following:

• A child with recurrent headaches, vomiting, and papilledema (swelling of the optic disc on funduscopic examination). These are symptoms and signs of raised intracranial pressure, which can be caused by brain tumor, brain edema or hemorrhage following head injury, and encephalopathy secondary to lead poisoning and other toxins. Cerebral tumor may rarely mimic the signs and symptoms of ADHD, and in patients presenting with headaches and incoordination, the diagnosis must always be considered. Blood lead levels sufficient to result in brain edema were relatively common before the 1970s, but lead abatement in recent years has prevented such severe complications. Lower levels of lead exposure may result in the symptoms of inattentiveness, hyperactivity and cognitive impairments.

• ADHD complicated by headaches or seizures and an abnormal EEG, especially if the epileptiform discharge or slowing is focal and localized in one hemisphere. An EEG showing left temporal slowing in a 7-year-old boy with a cystic swelling in the brain demonstrated on MRI is shown in Fig. 4-1. The child presented with ADHD and headaches.

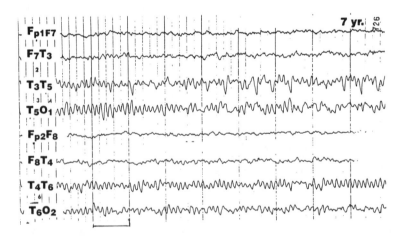

Figure 4-1. Electroencephalogram showing left temporal (T3T5) slow waves in a 7 year-old boy with ADHD and headaches, and a left temporal brain cyst demonstrated on MRI.

• ADHD complicated by language delay or aphasia

and seizures.

• ADHD and learning disablity associated with neurocutaneous syndromes, such as neurofibromatosis or Sturge-Weber syndrome.

MRI may require the younger child to be heavily sedated, and the indications for the test must be weighed against the associated risks.

Q: What blood tests may be advised?

A: Blood tests sometimes helpful in determining the cause or contributing factors in ADHD include the following:

• CBC to rule out anemia and iron deficiency.

• Blood lead level, especially in younger children with higher risks of exposure.

• Thyroid profile, T3, T4, TSH, to rule out thyroid dysfunction, especially in children with a family history of thyroid disease, or short stature.

• Chromosome analysis, especially in children with signs of fragile X disease.

None of these tests should be considered routine.

Q: What tests are mainly of research interest?

A: Parents will sometimes ask about tests used principally in research studies at university centers. These include positron emission tomography (PET) and SPECT, a similar test used to demonstrate changes in glucose metabolism in the frontal lobes of adults with a childhood history of ADHD. The test involves isotopes and is not advised in children.

Brainstem auditory evoked potentials (BAEPs) or responses (BAERs) show changes that may be used as tests for ADD and the differentiation of ADHD subtypes. Evoked potentials and quantitative EEG analysis have also been used to study cognitive impairments. Research-orientated laboratories are required for these types of studies and the evaluation of results.

Blood, urine, and spinal fluid measurements of neurotransmitters, norepinephrine and dopamine, show changes in some patients with ADHD, and these are modified by treatment with methylphenidate. The biochemical basis for ADHD is an interesting research topic but insufficiently documented for use in practice.

Q: What are some early risk factors for a diagnosis of ADHD in childhood?

A: The following factors may be predictive of the early development of ADHD before a child enters kindergarten:

- A family history of ADHD.
- A mother smoking or drinking alcohol during pregnancy.
- A mother addicted to cocaine during the pregnancy and neonatal period.
- Poor socio-economic status and low educational attainment of parents.
- Exposure to lead and elevated blood lead levels in infancy and early childhood.
- Delayed milestones of speech and language and psychomotor development.
- Early evidence of hyperactivity and irritability

during infancy.

• Exposure to unstructured and critical discipline practices and unstable emotional climate in the home.

TABLE 4-1. MILESTONES OF DEVELOPMENT IN INFANCY
    AND EARLY CHILDHOOD

AGE	MOTOR FUNCTIONS	COMMUNICATION
1st month	Infantile grasp reflex; Reflex stepping.	Blinks to light; Startles with noises.
4 months	Good head control; Shakes rattle.	Follows fully with eyes; Turns to sound.
6 months	Transfers objects; Rolls over on back.	Extends arms to be held; Responding to name.
8 months	Sits without support.	"Da-da" sounds.
9 months	Crawls; Stands with support; Picks up crumb with thumb and finger.	Plays "patty-cake;" Waves "bye-bye; Responds to "no."
1 year	Walks, one hand held.	Knows 2-4 words.
14 months	Walks alone.	Builds 2 block tower.
18 months	Feeds self.	Many single words.
2 years	Runs, kicks ball; Bunny hops.	2-3-word sentences; Knows name.
3 years	Rides tricycle.	Copies circle.
4 years	Walks up stairs.	Copies cross (X).
5 years	Walks tandem; Hops on one foot.	Copies square; Knows colors.
6 years	Rides bicycle.	Copies triangle.
7 years		Copies diamond.

REFERENCES

Gordon N. Neurological Problems in Childhood. Oxford,
    Butterworth-Heinemann, 1993.
Menkes JH. Textbook of Child Neurology, 3rd ed. Philadelphia,
    Lea & Febiger, 1985.
Millichap JG. Ed. Progress in Pediatric Neurology I, II, & III.
    Chicago, PNB Publishers, 1991, 94, & 97.
Paine RS, Oppe TE. Neurologic Examination of Children. Clin
    Dev Med Vol 20/21. Oxford, Spastics Society and
    Heinemann Med Publ, 1966.
Swaiman KF. Pediatric Neurology. Principles and Practice, 2nd
    ed, Vol 1. St Louis, Mosby, 1994.

CHAPTER 5

LEARNING AND LANGUAGE DISABILITIES

Learning and language disabilities frequently complicate attention deficit disorders, and their recognition and remediation are essential for the successful management of ADHD. The essentials of learning were once defined as *reading, writing and arithmetic.* Specific learning disorders that involve the "three Rs" are termed dyslexia, dysgraphia and dyscalculia. Dyslexia or reading disability is the prototype of learning disabilities. Speech and language disorders include dysarthrias, or disorders of articulation, and aphasias or dysphasias, inabilities to comprehend and use language despite normal hearing and intellect.

Q: How is dyslexia defined and recognized?

A: *Dyslexia* is a disorder manifested by a difficulty in learning to read despite conventional instruction, adequate intelligence, and socio-cultural opportunity. It is dependent upon fundamental cognitive disabilities which are frequently of constitutional origin (World Federation of Neurology definition, Waites, 1968).

More current definitions, accepted by the International Dyslexia Association, include the following: *Dyslexia* is a neurologically-based, often familial, disorder, which interferes with the acquisition and processing of language. *Dyslexia* is one of several distinct learning disabilities. It is a specific language-based disorder of constitutional origin characterized by difficulties in single word decoding that reflect insufficient phonological processing.

Earlier suggestions that dyslexia is due to an immaturity of cerebral function are supported by MRI evidence of developmental cerebral anomalies (Galaburda AM et al, 1985). The anatomical location of these anomalies correlates with a "phonological-linguistic," or deficient speech sound and decoding basis for dyslexia (Denckla MB, 1994), rather than an alternative theory that proposes a defect in the visual system and perception of letters and words.

The left temporal-parietal area appears to be most critical in location of normal reading ability, but additional areas of the left hemisphere may be involved also. Some reports of acquired dyslexia following surgery on the brain have involved the left frontal lobe. A "disconnection theory" involving impaired relays between the anterior and posterior areas of the left brain has been proposed.

Dyslexia occurs in 5 to 10% of school children, at all levels of intelligence, from superior to low normal. Dyslexia may be an isolated abnormality or may be associated with other learning disabilities. Reading and spelling disability overlaps with ADHD and shows similar genetic characteristics but different brain localizations. Anatomically, left hemisphere deficits underly reading and other learning disabilities, whereas the right frontal lobe is involved in ADHD.

Q: What are the early signs of dyslexia?

A: The dyslexic child is able to learn simple words by rote memory or by association with pictures or other cues but makes frequent errors in pronunciation and often substitutes words of similar meanings. The most frequent signs of dyslexia are as follows:
- Failure to distinguish mirror-image letters, "d" and "b" and the words "big" and "dig."
- Reversal of letters, eg. "was" for "saw."
- Substitutions, eg. "bed" for "bad."
- Omissions, eg. "soon" for "spoon."
- Extra phonemes, eg. "open" for "pen."

The reading level is determined by standard tests such as the Jastak test of word recognition and pronunciation and Gray's oral reading paragraphs.

Q: What is the genetic factor in reading disability?

A: The strong predilection for boys is well documented but the method of genetic transmission of dyslexia is less well defined. Nancy Millichap, in her thesis on dyslexia (1986), reviewed studies of twins and found evidence in support of a genetic influence. Of a total of 96 twin pairs reported in the literature, 36 (88%) monozygotic twins were concordant for dyslexia compared to only 16 (29%) dizygotic twins. Between 25 and 50% of children with reading disability show an hereditary influence, with autosomal dominant, sex-linked recessive, and polygenetic transmission. The genetic pattern depends in part on the definition and the association with other learning disabilities in the families studied.

A subsequent twin study at the Hospital for Sick Children, London, UK, showed that genetic factors played a moderate role in reading retardation and a stronger influence in spelling disability (Stevenson J et al, 1987). A recent twin study at the University of New South Wales, Australia, involved children with ADHD complicated by reading and speech problems. Male twins were affected more frequently than female, and the reading disability in male twins became more severe in adolescence while that in female twins showed improvement (Levy F et al, 1996).

Q: What is the evidence for a neuro-anatomical basis for dyslexia?

A: Since the original Harvard University study showing cerebral developmental anomalies in CT scans of four dyslexic male subjects (Galaburda AM et al, 1985), the findings have been confirmed at autopsy in three women with dyslexia. Microscopic scars in the brains were linked to lupus erythematosus in the mother, and an immune mechanism for dyslexia was proposed (Humphreys P et al, 1990). Left-handedness was more important than immune disorders in a study of associated factors in dyslexic children at the Center for Reading Research, Stavanger, Norway (Tonnessen FE et al, 1993).

A reappraisal of the anatomical basis for dyslexia using MRI studies at Yale University School of Medicine, New Haven, CT, concluded that differences in sex, age, handedness, and the definition of dyslexia could explain discrepancies in brain region volumes in children with dyslexia and other learning disabilities (Schultz RT et al, 1994). A small corpus callosum was a further cerebral anomaly discovered in MRI studies of dyslexic children at the University of Georgia, Augusta (Hynd GW et al, 1995). Familial left-handedness and ADHD distinguished the dyslexic children from control children in the study. Measurements of the corpus callosum in genetic studies of twin pairs at Dartmouth Medical School (1989) showed greater conformity and might be more reliable in dyslexic studies (Millichap, JG, 1997).

MRI and CT measurements of brain regions in dyslexic subjects have provided evidence of anomalies suggesting interruptions in brain development, possibly related to immune mechanisms. These studies are investigational and the anomalies are not sufficiently well documented to be used in diagnosis.

In addition to studies of the neuroanatomy of developmental dyslexia in subjects born with the disorder, occasional cases are described in adults with acquired dyslexia who have undergone surgery for cerebral tumor or other discretely localized brain lesions. A right-handed woman, a patient at the

University of Iowa College of Medicine, developed severe dyslexia and dysgraphia following the surgical removal of a small tumor located in the left premotor frontal lobe. By contrast, she was able to write numbers and perform written calculations without difficulty. The isolated simultaneous occurrence of dyslexia and dysgraphia, without dyscalculia, is rare. This case-report suggests that the frontal lobe of the brain may be involved in some cases of dyslexia (Anderson SW et al, 1990). Figs. 5-1 and 5-2 (pp 82, 83) show the anatomy of language and areas of representation of dyslexia, dysgraphia, dyscalculia and dysphasia.

Q: What are the newer brain imaging scanners used in dyslexia research?

A: The PET (Positron-emission tomography) scanner, developed in 1974, provides images of brain metabolic activity using radioactive tracer isotopes, but the technique is expensive and the resolution blurry. Newer PET scanners are being developed with improved sensitivity. Radiologists using PET scanners inject water containing the isotope oxygen-15 into the blood-stream, and the positrons emitted by the isotope produce energy that is picked up by radiation detectors on the scalp. The resulting images are color coded by computers and reflect areas of increased blood flow.

The fMRI (Functional magnetic resonance imaging), a more sensitive scanner than PET, also relies on an increase in cerebral blood flow to show changes in brain cell activity in various locations. Both these machines demonstrate regional changes within seconds whereas nerve cells transmit messages in milliseconds. Neither the PET nor the fMRI will determine the order and timing of processes involved in the recognition of letters and words.

Magnetoencephalography (MEG) is employed to track noninvasively in milliseconds the brain activation sequences during reading. The EEG detects electrical currents in the brain, while the MEG promptly records the magnetic effects of these currents. The fMRI can be used for localization of the brain activity during reading and MEG for the timing of the process, a spatial-temporal measuring device, or magnetic source imaging.

Q: What brain regions are activated during reading?

A: Magnetic source imaging (MSI), a combination of magnetoencephalography (MEG) and the anatomic images on MRI, has been used to provide anatomic location of brain activity at a given time, during reading by dyslexics and normal readers. In a study at the University of Helsinki, Finland, dyslexics failed to activate the left visual and receptive language cortical areas during word presentation, but instead, activated the left inferior frontal lobe (Salmelin R et al, 1996).

An impaired perception of visual word processing of written words resulted from a dysfunction of auditory language areas in the left temporal lobe. The activation of the left posterior temporal lobe during reading aloud or silently has been observed in PET studies of normal readers examined at the Hammersmith Hospital, London (Price CJ et al, 1994). The most critical neuroanatomic area of dysfunction in dyslexic subjects is the left posterior temporal, a region of the brain that governs the understanding of spoken words and also transmits visual perception fiber tracts.

Q: Is dyslexia a visual pathway disorder?

A: A number of highly sophisticated studies including visual evoked potentials have pointed to deficits in the visualization of letters and whole words in some dyslexics. Scientists from the Research Laboratory of Electronics and the Departments of Biology, Electrical Engineering and Computer Science at MIT, Cambridge, MA, have collaborated in an investigation of the peripheral and central vision of 5 dyslexic adult subjects compared to 5 normal readers. Dyslexics have impairments of letter discrimination in the central field of vision and better than normal peripheral vision for letter identification. After a program of exercises involving spatial organization and eye-hand coordination and the use of a device to utilize peripheral vision in reading, the recognition of letters by severe dyslexics was significantly improved. Dyslexics should be taught to read using peripheral vision (Geiger G, Lettvin JY, 1987).

Slowing of visual evoked responses in reading-disabled children has been demonstrated at the School of Optometry, University of Missouri, St Louis (Lehmkuhle S et al, 1993). MEG and MRI studies also point to involvement of cerebral visual pathways and function as well as receptive language centers. Although a so-called "phonolinguistic" theory of dyslexia (inability to recognize and decode speech sounds or phonemes) is favored, deficits in the visualization of words appear to be important in some dyslexic subjects. These two types of dyslexia have been termed *dysphonetic and dyseidetic* (Boder E, 1973). Dysphonetic dyslexics compensate by becoming visual spellers, while dyseidetic dyslexics use auditory pathways and phonics. The Lehtinen multisensory approach to remedial reading, developed for hyperactive children with ADD, is reviewed by Millichap N (1986).

Q: What are the articulatory feedback and disconnection theories of dyslexia?

A: Researchers at the University of Florida, Gainesville, FL, have proposed a motor-articulatory feedback hypothesis to explain developmental dyslexia (Heilman KM et al, 1996). The authors theorize that most children learn to read by the alphabetic system, requiring speech sound (phonological) awareness and conversion of letters (graphemes) into speech sounds (phonemes). Most dyslexics have deficient phonological awareness and difficulty converting graphemes into phonemes. The left inferior frontal lobe, involved in articulation, is important in phonological reading, as demonstrated in PET studies. Dyslexic children are unable to perceive the position and movement of the articulatory muscles (mouth, lips, tongue) during speech. Their phonological awareness and ability to convert graphemes to phonemes is impaired. Deficits in programming or feedback of motor articulation are related to this lack of awareness of the muscles of articulation.

A "disconnection" theory involving impaired relays

between anterior and posterior language areas of the brain is proposed by investigators at the MRC Cognitive Development Unit, London, UK (Paulesu E et al, 1996). Using PET to study brain activity in 5 adults with developmental dyslexia, left hemisphere brain regions normally activated in phonological processing were defective.

Q: How are reading remediation methods sometimes selected for individual dyslexics?

A: Subtyping of dyslexic children proposed by Boder (1973) has been validated by neurophysiological tests and may be used in the choice of remediation methods (Flynn JM, Deering WM, 1989). In a study at the Gunderson Clinic, LaCrosse, WI, dyslexic subgroups, *dysphonetic* (with auditory-phonetic disabilities) and *dyseidetic* (visual-spatial disabilities), showed significant differences on tests of reading and in EEG activity over the left temporal-parietal, angular gyrus, an area involved in phonetic decoding. This area showed overuse or increased activity in the dyseidetic children who audibly decoded words, whereas dysphonetic dyslexics skipped unknown words or substituted words with the same beginning sound.

The Boder test is based on the premise that dyslexic readers have characteristic patterns of strengths and weaknesses in two distinct cognitive components of the reading process: 1) the visual gestalt function, and 2) the auditory analytic function. The visual gestalt function underlies the ability to develop a sight vocabulary. The auditory analytic function governs phonic word-analysis skills. These two cognitive functions are basic to the two standard methods of initial reading instruction: 1) the whole word method and 2) the phonic method. The Boder test results are helpful to the educator in the choice of remediation methods. The matching method or *neuropsychological approach* to reading remediation involves matching the learning strengths with a teaching strategy designed to exploit these strengths. This matching method appears to be theoretically sound and much preferred to techniques based on deficit remediation, involving the training or retraining of damaged or dysfunctional areas of the brain.

Q: What alternative methods of reading remediation have been promoted and what is the prognosis for the child with dyslexia?

A: A wide variety of methods of reading remediation have been recommended, beginning with the multisensory (phonetic-kinesthetic) technique described by Orton (1937), Gillingham and Stillman (1940), Fernald (1943), and Strauss and Lehtinen (1947). An excellent review of these and other methods is provided by Millichap N (1986).

The multisensory method is included in the category known as the "one best method" or VAKT, which stands for visual, auditory, kinesthetic and tactile stimulation. In learning a word by the VAKT approach, the child sees the word, hears the teacher say the word, and simultaneously says the word himself, traces it, and feels the muscle movement and touch sensation in his fingers.

Critics of the multisensory approach are concerned

about the rigidity of the teaching method, the tendency to belabor reading, and the lack of emphasis on comprehension. The emphasis on phonics precludes its application with dysphonetic dyslexic children or those weak in auditory perception.

Another category of remedial reading focused on remediation of prerequisite reading readiness skills that are presumed lacking in the dyslexic child. Proponents (Kephart, Frostig, Doman-Delacato, and Kirk) theorized that perceptual motor, cerebral dominance, and psycholinguistic skills need to be developed as a foundation for reading readiness. Critics argue that the treatment methods lack proof of effectiveness, and techniques based on deficit remediation may lead to poor self-concept and negative attitudes toward reading and school in general (Hynd, Cohen, 1983; Hartlage, 1981).

Alternatives to the deficit remediation methods are those that determine each child's intact areas of neurological functioning and match cognitive neuropsychological strengths with a teaching strategy designed to exploit these strengths. This matching method, sometimes termed the neuropsychological approach to reading remediation, is favored by experts including Johnson and Myklebust, Boder, and Mattis. A battery of psychological tests to assess the child's cognitive abilities is a prerequisite to the choice of method of reading remediation. Those with stronger phono-linguistic abilities are taught by the phonic and decoding methods, and those with weak phonic abilities and normal visual-spatial function may respond better to a look-say, whole-word or a multisensory approach.

Dyslexic children often come to the remedial setting

after several years of frustration due to poor academic success in the regular classroom. The child's self concept is low, and he may have attention deficit hyperactivity disorder. A reconditioning period is often advisable, during which behavior modification is employed along with medications to improve attention.

Under favorable conditions most dyslexic children can be taught to read by appropriate remedial methods, but a minority of severely disabled children remain illiterate despite all efforts made by qualified tutors. The ability to read should not be confused with intelligence, and poor readers are not necessarily poor learners. Indeed, some dyslexic children have entered professions and have enjoyed success in adult life by compensating for their disability. The relative importance of reading in learning may need to be de-emphasized and alternative channels such as audiovisual materials employed to teach children with severe dyslexia refractory to therapy.

WRITING AND ARITHMETIC LEARNING DISORDERS

Q: What is dysgraphia?

A: Dysgraphia, or agraphia, is an inability to write or print words and numbers in the absence of paralysis of the arm or hand. It is esentially an apraxia involving the hand.

Mild cases may be manifested by contraction of words, elision of letters or syllables, poor spacing of letters and words or mirror writing. Dysgraphia often complicates aphasia and dyslexia. Anatomically, the hand area is called Exner's writing center, located in the middle frontal convolution of the left frontal lobe (Fig. 5-1). Dysgraphia may also follow a posterior cerebral lesion and may be part of the Gerstmann syndrome (Fig. 5-2).

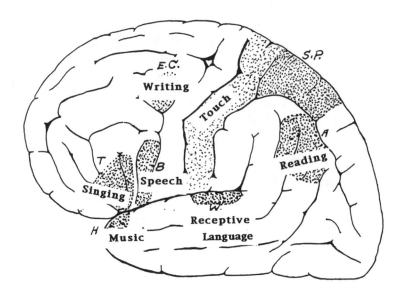

Figure 5-1. Diagrammatic outline of language centers (shaded) in the left dominant cerebral hemisphere.
A=angular gyrus, important in reading, spelling and writing; EC=Exner's writing center; B=Broca's motor speech area; W=Wernicke's receptive language area. Various language centers are interrelated with each other and with other parts of the brain. (Modified from Nielsen JM. Agnosia, Apraxia, Aphasia. New York, Paul B Hoeber, Inc, 1965, with permission).

Q: What is the Gerstmann syndrome?

A: Gerstmann syndrome consists of the following disabilities, as shown in Fig. 5-2:

• *Finger agnosia,* or an inability to recognize, name or select individual fingers of the hand.

• *Right-left disorientation,* or confused laterality.

• *Agraphia,* or an inability to write.

• *Acalculia,* an inability to count or to understand arithmetical problems.

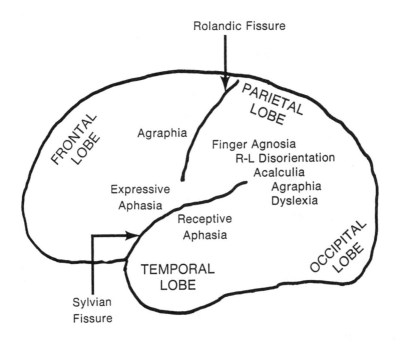

Figure 5-2. Diagram of left cerebral hemisphere showing the neuroanatomic localizations of lesions causing disorders of language and learning.

Gerstmann syndrome has been described in adults with tumors and stroke lesions involving the angular gyrus, in the temporo-parietal cortex of the dominant hemisphere. Partial syndromes may occur with localized lesions of other cerebral cortical regions or even with diffuse cerebral pathology. Gerstmann syndrome occurs in children with ADHD who have learning disorders affecting hand writing and arithmetic.

Q: What is meant by dyscalculia and what is the basis for arithmetical disability?

A: Dyscalculia is an inability to learn arithmetic and do simple arithmetical calculations. A child's development of numerical concepts begins as early as one year of age with his manipulation of one object after another. As a prerequisite to counting he gains insight into concepts of size, number and form by playing with form boards, puzzles and boxes. He learns about sequence and order by stringing beads or putting pegs in boards, and he adds to his ideas of quantity by learning phrases such as "all gone," "no more," and "too much."

Mathematical concepts include receptive and expressive aspects just as other forms of symbolic language, and modern methods of teaching mathematics emphasize meaning rather than rote learning. A child with dyscalculia is unable to understand mathematical principles and processes, but in addition, he may have difficulty revisualizing numbers, writing numbers, or understanding and remembering instructions. An auditory receptive language disorder will not affect arithmetical computation, but math involving reasoning and vocabulary will be weakened. Deficits in auditory memory and recall of numbers interfere with a child's mathematical performance because he cannot listen and assimilate all of the facts presented orally. Oral work should be minimized when auditory memory is impaired.

Dyslexia and visual perceptual disturbances resulting in confusion of letters may interfere with the ability to read and understand mathematical problems but do not impair calculation when problems are read aloud. Dyslexic children have little difficulty in learning arithmetic when presented with numerical symbols, but they are unable to solve problems in which the written word is used instead.

Children with dysgraphia may have difficulty in writing numerals as well as words. The use of problems with multiple-choice answers that can be encircled or underlined will prevent arithmetical failure due to apraxic disorders.

At the Schneider Children's Medical Center, Jerusalem, Israel, an 11 year-old, Hebrew-speaking boy of normal intelligence was referred for evaluation of learning and attentional problems and was found to have a profound dyscalculia based on a proposed lack of "cardinal/ordinal skills acquisition device" (COSAD). Several male family members had dysgraphia, right-left disorientation, and dyslexia. At birth, the child was hypotonic, and motor development was delayed, walking independently at 2 and 1/2 years.

Neurologic abnormalities included high-pitched voice, dysgraphia, right-left disorientation, finger agnosia, clumsiness in running and jumping, scoliosis, and fine motor incoordination. At 4 years, he developed grand mal seizures treated with carbamazepine, and at 7 years he received pemoline (Cylert) for ADD without hyperactivity. The pemoline benefited overall functioning. The use of linguistic, visual and verbal memory cues compensated for deficits in ordinal number use, but not for cardinal number skills, which remained limited. He could count small numbers, but could not do simple calculations, a skill requiring an innate experience of quantity, less amenable to language, visuo-spatial, or logical mediation (Ta'ir J et al, 1997).

Profound developmental dyscalculia and Gerstmann's syndrome may occur in children of normal or even superior intelligence. Deficits in specific cognitive areas may involve visuo-spatial perception and parietal-occipital dysfunction. In a theoretical hypothesis of developmental dyscalculia, an innate, highly specific cognitive domain is involved. Ordinal number tasks and counting small magnitudes may be successfully completed, whereas larger quantities involving calculations are not possible.

Q: Are girls with ADHD more prone to learning impairments than boys?

A: Girls with ADHD have a relatively greater tendency to inattention than hyperactivity-impulsivity, whereas neuropsychological deficits involving executive function, the ability to organize and monitor thoughts and behavior, are less remarkable in girls than in boys. Compared to normal controls, girls with ADHD are significantly more impaired on tests of attention, intellectual performance, and achievement, and have higher rates of learning disability. However, impairments of cognitive function, attention, arithmetic and reading are common to both sexes affected by ADHD (Seidman LJ et al, 1997).

SPEECH AND LANGUAGE DISORDERS

Q: What are the steps in normal development of speech and language?

A: An infant says his first intelligible word by about 1 year of age. During the second year the child recognizes the names of familiar objects and parts of the body and begins to form short phrases. In the third year he uses speech for toilet needs and social interaction in play, and at 4 years he can repeat songs and nursery rhymes. A useful index of a child's developmemt of language is the length of his responses when he is presented with familiar pictures or toys:

2 years old : 2-word responses
3 years old : 4 words
5 years old : 6 words
8 years old : 8 words

Q: What are the signs of language delay?

A: A delay in saying the first word beyond 18 months may indicate a physical, mental or hearing disability. Hearing should be checked in early infancy, especially if the child suffers from repeated ear infections or a family member has a hearing problem.

Failure to put 2 or 3 words together in short phrases by 2 years and sentences by the age of 3 years is a sign of significant language delay.

If the disability involves the neuromuscular control of speech and articulation, it is called *dysarthria.* When a child is unable to understand or use

language in the absence of deafness or mental
retardation, the term *aphasia* or *dysphasia* is used.

Q: What are the main types of aphasia and results of treatment?

A: The term *congenital aphasia* (or dysphasia) is
applied to the language deficit that is "developmental"
and is recognized in the first year or two of life.
Acquired aphasia presents after the acquisition of
language has begun, and results from lesions in the
language areas of the brain.

Aphasia acquired by children is usually reversible
if the cause is localized and nonprogressive, as with
trauma related lesions. The opposite hemisphere of the
brain assumes the function of the dominant side. In
adults, acquired aphasia is either permanent or
resolves slowly and incompletely in response to
therapy. Childhood aphasia due to infection, vascular
disease or that associated with epilepsy has a poor
outcome (Loonen MCB, van Dongen HR, 1990). *Epileptic
aphasia*, or Landau-Kleffner syndrome, is an acquired
form of aphasia that affects children with epilepsy and
develops between 2 and 5 years of age.

Aphasias are also classified as *expressive, receptive,*
or *expressive-receptive.* Expressive aphasia is an
apraxia, or loss of purposeful movements of the muscles
of speech or writing in the absence of paralysis.
Receptive aphasia is a visual and auditory agnosia, or
inability to interpret or comprehend the significance
of written or spoken words despite normal vision and
hearing. In *amnesic* or *nominal* aphasia the child has
difficulty in finding the name of an object although he

understands its purpose and correct usage.

The differentiation of aphasia from mental retardation or infantile autism may be difficult, but the aphasic child's general performance and facial expressive communication are more adequately developed and well in advance of his language performance.

Six syndromes of developmental dysphasia and their remediation were identified at the International Child Neurology Congress held in Jerusalem, Israel, 1986. The differentiation of subtypes of developmental and acquired dysphasias in young children has been facilitated by the MRI, which sometimes uncovers subtle cerebral anomalies. Some syndromes result from genetic neurodevelopmental abnormalities while others are caused by acquired lesions before or at birth. The authors theorize that early therapeutic intervention may stimulate brain reorganization and development of alternative pathways (Allen DA et al, 1989).

The language growth in 26 two year old children with expressive language delay was studied at the State University of New York, Stony Brook, NY (Fischel JE et al, 1989). After a 5 month follow-up period, improvement was variable, with 1/3 showing no improvement, 1/3 mild improvement, and 1/3 having normal language development. Predictors of improvement included the child's 2 year vocabulary size used at home, regular meal times, and the extent of quiet interaction between mother and child. The effectiveness of early intervention programs for language development outside the home was generally disappointing. More accurate diagnosis of subtypes of dysphasia might lead to more specific intervention techniques with more effective results.

Developmental dysphasia may be complicated by ADHD, adding to the problems of treatment.

A 7 year-old girl with developmental dysphasia, examined at the Medical College of Georgia, Augusta, GA, had been treated with methylphenidate for ADHD. She had said her first words late at 2 years and short phrases at 4 years of age. Her 6 year-old brother had developmental dyslexia of the dysphonetic type. Speech and language evaluations at 3 years showed no expressive language and wishes were communicated by pointing and gesturing. Receptive language was at an 18 month level and play audiometry revealed normal hearing. Her intelligence level was 70. In contrast to weaknesses in language and vocabulary development, her visual spatial perception and construction were relatively strong. A neurodevelopmental anomaly affecting the left frontal cortex was diagnosed, and a genetic basis for the language delay was suggested by the family history of learning disability (Cohen M et al, 1989).

Q: What new methods of treatment for aphasia have been developed?

A: An exciting new method using acoustically-modified synthetic speech has been introduced by researchers at Rutgers University, Newark, NJ, and University of California, San Francisco, CA (Tallal P, Merzenich MM et al, 1996). Deficits in recognition and processing of rapidly successive phonetic elements of speech in language impaired children, aged 5 to 10 years, were improved by listening to synthetic speech presented at at a slower rate on audiotapes and by daily training with computer games designed to modify phoneme perception. After 1 month of daily training exercises, test scores improved by 2 years, and normal levels of speech discrimination and language comprehension were achieved. Compared to a control group of language-learning impaired children receiving natural speech training, those treated with acoustically-modified speech training showed significantly larger improvements. If confirmed, this method of language training intervention will improve the outcome of developmental dysphasias.

REFERENCES

Allen DA, Mendelson L, Rapin I. Syndrome specific remediation in preschool developmental dysphasia. In Child Neurol and Dev Disabilities. French JH et al (eds), Baltimore, Brookes, 1989.

Anderson SW, Demasio AR, Demasio H. Troubled letters but not numbers. Domain specific cognitive impairments following damage in frontal cortex. Brain 1990;113:749-766.

Boder E. Developmental dyslexia: A diagnostic approach used on three atypical reading-spelling patterns. Dev Med Child Neurol 1973;15:663-687.

Cohen M et al. Neuropathological abnormalities in developmental dysphasia. Ann Neurol 1989;25:567-570.

Denckla MB. Introduction to Learning Disorders. In: Progress in Pediatric Neurology II, Ed. Millichap JG, Chicago, PNB Publishers, 1994.

Flynn JM, Deering WM. Subtypes of dyslexia: Investigation of Boder's system using quantitative neurophysiology. Dev Med Child Neurol 1989;31:215-223.

Galaburda AM et al. Developmental dyslexia: Four consecutive patients with cortical anomalies. Ann Neurol 1985;18:222.

Geiger G, Lettvin JY. Peripheral and central vision of dyslexic adults. N Engl J Med 1987;316:1238.

Hartlage LC. Neuropsychological assessment techniques. In Reynolds CR, Gutkin TB (eds). The Handbook of School Psychology. New York, Wiley, 1981.

Heilman KM et al. Developmental dyslexia: a motor-articulatory feedback hypothesis. Ann Neurol 1996;39:407-412.

Humphreys P et al. Developmental dyslexia in women: Neuropathological findings in three patients. Ann Neurol 1990;28:727-738.

Hynd G, Cohen M. Dyslexia. Neuropsychological Theory, Research, and Clinical Differentiations. New York, Grune & Stratton, 1983.

Hynd GW et al. Dyslexia and corpus callosum morphology. Arch Neurol 1995;52:32-38.

Lehmkuhle S et al. A defective visual pathway in children with reading disability. N Engl J Med 1993;328:989-996.

Levy F et al. Twin-sibling differences in ADHD children with reading and speech problems. J Child Psychol Psychiatry 1996;37:569-578.

Loonen MCB, van Dongen HR. Acquired childhood aphasia. Outcome 1 year after onset. Arch Neurol 1990;47:1324-1328.

Merzenich MM et al. Temporal processing deficits of language-learning impaired children ameliorated by training. Science 1996;271:77-81.

Millichap NM. Dyslexia: Theories of Causation and Methods of Management. An Historical Perspective. Loyola University of Chicago, Masters Degree Thesis, 1986.

Millichap NM, Millichap JG. Dyslexia: As the Educator and Neurologist Read It. Springfield, IL, Charles C Thomas, 1986.

Millichap JG. Ed. Progress in Pediatric Neurology III. Chicago,

PNB Publishers, 1997.

Nielsen JM. Agnosia, Apraxia, Aphasia. Their Value in Cerebral Localization. New York, Hafner Publ Comp, Paul B Hoeber, 1965.

Paulesu E et al. A disconnection syndrome hypothesis for developmental dyslexia. Brain 1996;119:143-157.

Price CJ et al. Brain activity during reading. The effects of exposure duration and task. Brain 1994;117:1255-1269.

Salmelin R et al. Impaired visual word processing in dyslexia revealed with magnetoencephalography. Ann Neurol 1996;40:157-162.

Schultz RT et al. Brain morphology in normal and dyslexic children: The influence of sex and age. Ann Neurol 1994;35:732-742.

Seidman LJ et al. A pilot study of neuropsychological function in girls with ADHD. J Am Acad Child Adolesc Psychiatry 1997;36:366-373.

Stevenson J et al. A twin study of genetic influences on reading and spelling ability and disability. J Child Psychol Psychiat 1987;28:229-247.

Ta'ir J et al. Profound developmental dyscalculia: evidence for a cardinal/ordinal skills acquisition device. Brain and Cognition 1997;35:184-206.

Tallal P et al. Language comprehension in language-learning impaired children improved with acoustically modified speech. Science 1996;271:81-84.

Tonnessen FE et al. Dyslexia, left-handedness, and immune disorders. Arch Neurol 1993;50:411-416.

World Federation of Neurology Definition. In Waites L. Definition of dyslexia. Can Med Assoc J 1968;99:37.

CHAPTER **6**

TICS, TOURETTE SYNDROME, SEIZURES, AND HEADACHES

Neurologic disorders that sometimes complicate the syndrome of attention deficit hyperactivity disorder include **tics and Tourette syndrome, seizures and headaches.** Causes underlying the ADHD may also be responsible for these symptoms or, alternatively, drugs used in the treatment of ADHD may result in neurologic side-effects. Special tests, including an EEG and CT or MRI, may be necessary to uncover the cause and determine the appropriate therapy. The recognition and diagnosis of associated neurologic disorders is important for the optimal management of ADHD.

Q: How are tics and Tourette syndrome recognized?

A: A tic or habit spasm is an involuntary, recurrent twitch or motor movement (motor tic) or a grunt or vocalization (vocal tic). *Simple motor tics* involve the eyes, as in eye-blinking (blepharospasm), the face (grimacing) and the head, neck and shoulders (jerking, twisting and shrugging movements). *Simple vocal tics* include throat-clearing, grunting, sniffing and barking. *Complex motor tics* are gestures, jumping and touching objects. *Complex vocal tics* are utterances of obscene language (coprolalia), repeating words or phrases, sometimes out of context (palilalia), and repeating words said by another person (echolalia). Sometimes precipitated by a physical or emotional stimulus, the tic can be controlled partially by will and is infrequent during sleep. It is exaggerated by stress and fatigue and lessened by diverting the child's attention.

Tics can be *transient* or *chronic,* and *definite* (observed by the physician) or only by *history or report* (not observed by the physician). *Transient tic disorder* lasts for at least two weeks, but no longer than one year. *Chronic tic disorder* is manifested by either motor or vocal tics, but not both, occurring intermittently for more than one year.

Tourette syndrome, named after a French neurologist, Georges Gilles de la Tourette, is characterized by chronic tics, both motor and vocal, persisting for longer than one year. Tourette first described his syndrome in 1885, with a preliminary report in 1884. An English-language translation of the report is provided by Lajonchere C et al (1996).

Q: How prevalent is Tourette syndrome among school children?

A: The incidence of reported cases of Tourette syndrome (TS) before the 1960s was low, and the disorder was generally omitted from the index of textbooks of neurology. Increased public awareness of TS and the recognition of organic in addition to functional psychiatric causes have led to an increase in apparent prevalence. The frequency of transient tics in childhood is variably quoted at 4% to 16%. A study involving school children from Monroe County, NY, conducted at the University of Rochester Medical Center, NY, detected 41 with Tourette syndrome (TS), with an estimated prevalence of 29 per 100,000 (Caine ED et al, 1988).

In the Monroe County study, TS was a mild disorder in more than one half the cases, and medication was required in less than half. Thirty-seven were boys and four were girls. Eleven (27%) had ADHD, and methylphenidate appeared to be the cause in 10 (25%). In addition to simple motor and vocal tics, 20 (50%) children had complex vocalizations including coprolalia, echolalia and stuttering. Twenty (50%) also had obsessive compulsive symptoms, including touching or repetitive placing of objects.

The remarkably large percentage of patients with TS related to ADHD and treatment with methylphenidate (25% in this series) might explain the increased awareness of Tourette syndrome since the 1960s, when the use of Ritalin® became widespread. A questionnaire mailed to pediatric neurologists to determine their usage of methylphenidate in the treatment of ADHD revealed that 5% of children who were treated with methylphenidate developed tics (Millichap JG, 1997).

Q: What are the causes of tics and Tourette syndrome?

A: Originally considered an emotional, compulsive or psychiatric disorder, recent research emphasizes an organic, neurologic basis for tic disorders. Both genetic and acquired factors are invoked. Acquired causes include encephalitis, head trauma, neonatal asphyxia, and an abnormal reaction to streptococcal infection. Congenital anomalies of brain development have been demonstrated in some cases, and tics in adults can occur rarely as manifestations of cerebral tumors, multiple sclerosis, Huntington's, Alzheimer's and Creutzfeldt-Jakob diseases.

In children with ADHD, tics may be precipitated by stimulant medications such as methylphenidate (Ritalin®), amphetamines (Dexedrine,® Adderal®), or pemoline (Cylert®). Dietary stimulants including coffee, tea and chocolate may also exacerbate tics. A neurochemical mechanism for the stimulant-induced tic seems likely. Methylphenidate is probably the most common precipitating cause of tics and Tourette syndrome among school age children.

Other factors found to influence the frequency and severity of tics include hormonal changes, thermal stress, voluntary and purposeful compulsions, and stimulus-induced behaviors or "impulsions." Menstrual cycle fluctuations in the frequency of tics were noted in adolescent girls with Tourette syndrome followed at the Children's Hospital of Wisconsin, Milwaukee, WI (Schwabe MJ, Konkol RJ, 1992). Tics increased with menarche, the beginning of menstruation and before each menstrual period; they decreased after menstruation.

A 17 year-old boy with Tourette syndrome had more frequent tics during warmer weather, during fever, or after vigorous exercise (Lombroso PJ et al, 1991). In a study of patients' perceptions of tics, two thirds of a group of 60 patients diagnosed with Tourette syndrome thought their movements and vocalizations were intentional and under voluntary control. This perception of the nature of tics is contrary to the prevailing neurologic theory of an involuntary movement disorder, only partially controlled by will (Lang A, 1991). The term "impulsions" is used to describe tics and obsessive compulsive behaviorisms induced by stimuli such as tightness in the chest or tingling sensations (sensory tic) or in response to another person coughing (reflex tic) (Eapen V et al, 1994). .

Q: What is known about the genetics of Tourette syndrome and tic disorders?

A: An autosomal dominant mode of transmission from both maternal and paternal sides of the family is suggested by genetic studies, but the identification of a responsible gene remains elusive. Maternally transmitted cases have an earlier age of onset (Eapen V et al, 1997). Studies in monozygotic twins with tic disorders have shown a concordance rate of less than 100% and a variability of tic severity among family members, ranging from simple transient tic disorder to severe and persistent Tourette syndrome (TS). The TS gene is variably expressed as TS, transient tic disorder, or chronic tic disorder (Kurlan R et al, 1988).

Children with a first-degree relative with Tourette syndrome have an increased risk of developing tic disorders. and they are also more likely to have obsessive compulsive and attention deficit disorders (Carter AS et al, 1994). Environmental factors in addition to inheritance play a role in the causation of tics and TS, and the neurotransmitter dopamine is involved in the mechanism of these disorders.

Q: What structural brain abnormalities have been demonstrated by MRI studies in Tourette syndrome?

A: Reduction in volume and asymmetries in size of the basal ganglia, and increases in the size of certain regions of the corpus callosum have been defined by analysis of MRIs of children and adolescents with Tourette syndrome (TS). Using special imaging techniques, Singer HS, Denckla MB and colleagues at the Kennedy Krieger Institute, Johns Hopkins University, found in contrast to those with TS alone, children with TS and ADHD showed decreases in size of certain areas of the corpus callosum and changes involving different areas of the basal ganglia (1993, 1996). Tourette syndrome and ADHD may result from distinct neurodevelopmental processes, representing different degrees of expression of the same gene.

Acute basal ganglia enlargement was correlated with severity of obsessive compulsive disorder (OCD) and tics following a hemolytic streptococcal throat infection in a 12-year-old boy. Serum antibodies against the basal ganglia and antistreptolysin titers were elevated in children with ADHD complicated by tics or other movement disorders (Kiessling LS et al, 1993). Antibiotic and blood plasmapheresis treatments were followed by a rapid shrinking of the basal ganglia and improvement in the OCD and tics (Giedd JN, Rapoport JL et al, 1996). The swelling of the basal ganglia might be explained by an inflammation and edema (fluid collection) secondary to a reaction between antibodies and invading bacteria. Tics and OCD appear to represent in some cases an autoimmune reaction to streptococcal infection, and immunological and antibiotic therapies can be beneficial.

The neuroanatomical studies using MRI measurements show correlations between volume changes in the basal ganglia and corpus callosum and the severity of Tourette syndrome. These anatomical changes can be developmental and genetic and in some cases, result from infection and an autoimmune reaction. Other environmental factors altering the function of the basal ganglia and resulting in tics include head trauma and encephalitis.

Q: What is the relation of streptococcal infection to tics?

A: The association between Group A b-hemolytic streptococcal infection (GABHS) and the development of tics and Tourette syndrome (TS) has been called a pediatric autoimmune disorder, similar to Sydenham's chorea (SC) and rheumatic fever. The mechanism of SC and streptococcal-induced TS is related to GABHS antibodies cross-reacting with the basal ganglia and resulting in the characteristic movement disorders and antineuronal antibody formation. Tics and TS as a sequel to SC has been recognized for more than 60 years (Guttmann E (1927), in Wilson SAK, 1955), and the recently reported association of tics with streptococcal infection might be expected.

Tics with an autoimmune mechanism are often associated with obsessive compulsive disorder. Evidence of a recent streptococcal infection may include a history of sore-throat, sinusitis or flu-like symptoms, a positive throat culture, and positive antistreptolysin O titer. Treatment of tics with penicillin is dependent on a recent history of infection and elevated antistreptolysin titers. The use of antibiotics to prevent future exacerbations of tics is controversial and requires further study.

Q: What is the evidence for encephalitis as a cause of Tourette syndrome?

A: A six-year-old girl who developed a Tourette-like syndrome following herpes encephalitis was treated at Walter Reed Army Medical Center, Washington, DC, and Johns Hopkins University, Baltimore, MD (Northram RS, Singer HS, 1991). At two weeks after recovery from the encephalitis and discharge from hospital she developed eye blinking and sudden, rapidly recurrent, purposeless movements and vocalizations. The motor tics were characterized by facial grimacing, head twitching and shoulder shrugging plus eye rolling, facial contortions, jumping, touching objects and body parts and making obscene gestures. Vocal tics included grunting, sniffing, and snorting sounds. Recovery followed several weeks of therapy with pimozide (Orap®). MRIs showed a hemorrhage in the basal ganglia and temporal lobe of the brain. An EEG showed slow waves over the same temporal lobe region, indicating destruction or swelling of brain tissue.

Older textbooks of neurology refer to tics and Tourette-like syndrome as complications of encephalitis lethargica and, like the hyperactive behavior syndrome (ADHD), these movement disorders were a delayed result of the influenza epidemic of 1918. Opinions favored an organic, brain-damage cause for the encephalitis-induced tic, while other tic disorders unassociated with encephalitis were regarded as compulsive habit spasms and symptoms of psychogenic illness (Wilson, SA Kinnear, 1955). The more recent medical literature invokes encephalitis as just one of a number of acquired causes for Tourette syndrome.

Q: Do children with Tourette syndrome have an increased risk of learning disabilities?

A: In a study of 138 children with Tourette's syndrome (TS) at the University of Rochester, NY, a diagnosis of specific learning disorder was made in 30 (22%). Of the remaining 108, 36 (33%) had significant school problems, including grade retention and special education placement. The association of ADHD with TS was a significant predictor of academic problems (Abwender DA et al, 1996).

More than 50% of children with Tourette syndrome are affected by specific learning disabilities or other academic problems. Tics themselves are not the reason for the school problems, but rather the associated "comorbid" ADHD. These findings confirm those of the Johns Hopkins investigators, who report that children with TS complicated by ADHD have a 32% risk of developing a specific learning disability whereas those with TS alone have no academic problems (Schuerholz LJ et al, 1996).

Children with either TS or chronic tic disorder suffered from learning disabilities and lowered academic achievement, in a study at the Massachusetts General Hospital, Boston (Spencer T, Biederman J et al, 1995). They differed from control subjects in increased rates of comorbid ADHD, obsessive-compulsive disorder (OCD), mood disorders (depression, bipolar disorder), antisocial disorders (conduct and oppositional defiant disorder (ODD)), and anxiety disorders. TS patients differed from tic disorder patients in having higher rates of OCD and ODD. TS and chronic tic disorder are related diseases, TS being more severe than chronic tic disorder. Comorbidity with ADHD, occurring in 50% of TS patients, causes more disability than the motor tics.

Q: What is the risk of bipolar disorder among children with Tourette syndrome?

A: The incidence of bipolar disorder (manic or depressive symptoms) among children and adolescents with Tourette syndrome is four times higher than that expected by chance. Boys are at greater risk than girls, in a ratio of 5:1. The frequency and intensity of motor and vocal tics increase with manic symptoms and decrease with depressive symptoms. These findings were reported by the North Dakota Longitudinal Tourette Syndrome Surveillance Project, in which 205 patients were followed and 15 developed comorbid bipolar disorder, some with histories of ADHD (Kerbeshian J et al, 1995).

Common neurochemical mechanisms, involving noradrenergic, dopaminergic and serotonergic pathways in the basal ganglia, and genetic factors are invoked as explanations for the comorbidity of TS, bipolar disorder and ADHD.

Q: What treatments are available for tics and Tourette syndrome complicating ADHD?

A: If tics or Tourette syndrome occur in association with ADHD or are known to affect other members of the immediate family, stimulant medications and caffeine-containing drinks should be avoided. Children with ADHD who develop tics during treatment with methylphenidate or other stimulant should receive an alternative type of medication, such as the antihypertensive drug, clonidine. Before the introduction of clonidine, methylphenidate must be discontinued, since serious adverse reactions have been reported with the combined therapy.

Clonidine (Catapres®) is known pharmacologically as an a_2-adrenergic agonist. It lowers blood pressure by activating receptors in the brain stem, suppressing the outflow of sympathetic nervous system activity from the brain. The release of norepinephrine from peripheral nerve endings and the plasma concentration of norepinephrine are also decreased, effects that might explain the benefits observed in children with ADHD and tics.

In children of 5 years of age and older with ADHD

and tics, the usual starting dose is one half of a 0.1 mg tablet given by mouth at night, one hour before bedtime. Drowsiness is the most common side effect, and the dose may have to be modified to one quarter tablet nightly if drowsiness persists during the school day. Dryness of the mouth, occurring in 30 to 40% of adults taking clonidine, is rarely mentioned by children treated with the drug.

Unlike Ritalin, the response to clonidine is slow, often delayed for up to two weeks, and doses are given daily on school days and at weekends. Parents are warned to be patient, and teachers should not expect dramatic improvements in attention, focus or behavior when the drug is first introduced. After two weeks, one quarter tablet after breakfast is added daily if symptoms of ADHD and tics persist. Further increments in dosage are made slowly, usually at 7 day intervals and generally to a maximum of 0.15 mg daily, given in divided amounts 2 or 3 times a day, depending on the individual response and reports of drowsiness. The pulse and blood pressure should be monitored regularly, and withrawals of this drug should be slow, to prevent rebound in blood pressure. An electrocardiogram should be obtained before starting treatment, if cardiac problems are suspected.

It is unwise to combine clonidine with Ritalin, other stimulant medication, or tricyclic antidepressants. Serious side effects involving heart and blood pressure have occurred with these drug combinations, even fatalities.

A transdermal product is available, Catapres-TTS-1, which is applied to the skin of the upper arm, once every 7 days. Parents have sometimes requested the skin patch because of the ease of administration. Personally, I have had no experience with this form of clonidine and in general, I would not advise its use in children, except in tightly controlled and monitored conditions. About 15% to 20% of adult patients develop a skin rash or contact dermatitis when using the clonidine transdermal patch (Goodman and Gilman, 1996).

Guanfacine (Tenex®) is an alternative antihypertensive agent to clonidine, if clonidine is not tolerated or is found ineffective. The initial dosage in children of school age is one quarter to one half the 1.0 mg tablet daily, given one hour before bedtime. Drowsiness is the most common side effect, and increments in dosage of one quarter tablet are made slowly, at 7 to 14 day intervals, usually to a maximum of 1.5 mg daily in 2 or 3 divided amounts. The same precautions are observed with guanfacine as with clonidine.

In one study of guanfacine (1.5 mg daily) in 10 children with TS and ADHD, treated at Yale and Johns Hopkins Universities, significant improvements in attention were observed in continuous performance tasks, and the severity of motor and phonic tics was also decreased. Side effects included transient fatigue, headaches, and drowsiness (Chappell PB, Riddle MA et al, 1995).

Other medications sometimes advised in treatment of Tourette syndrome include risperidone, clomipramine, and haloperidol. Side effects must be monitored carefully, especially with haloperidol (Haldol), a treatment that I no longer recommend in children attending my clinic.

Children with transient tics rarely need medications. Parents are advised to withdraw caffeine-containing drinks and chocolate. The attention of the child should be diverted away from the recognition of the tics if possible, and anxiety-provoking situations at school and at home should be avoided. Chewing gum, found to allay anxiety and diminish the severity of tics, should be permitted by parents and teachers.

SEIZURES AND ADHD

Q: What types of seizures may occur with ADHD?

A: Seizures of the absence or complex partial types may be the cause of "daydreaming" or episodes of confusion and inattention noted by the teacher, psychologist or parent of a child with ADHD. An electroencephalogram (EEG) should be obtained in ADHD children with one or more of the following risk factors for seizures: 1) a history of convulsions in early childhood; 2) a history of epilepsy in a sibling or parent; 3) a history of head trauma, encephalitis or meningitis; or 4) episodes of staring, confusion, fear, uncontrolled rage or laughter.

Absence seizures are accompanied by a generalized EEG discharge whereas partial seizures originate with a focal, localized epileptiform discharge. An abnormal, epileptiform EEG might indicate a trial of antiepileptic medication before stimulants are prescribed for the ADHD.

Q: How frequent are EEG abnormalities with ADHD, and what is their significance in treatment?

A: EEGs in 100 children with ADHD studied consecutively in my clinic showed abnormal discharges compatible with epilepsy in 7%. Another 19% had moderate irregularities indicative of brain dysfunction, not specific for epilepsy (Millichap JG, 1977). An abnormal EEG is not always an indication for antiepileptic (AED) therapy, but when associated with episodic symptoms suggestive of seizures, a trial of AED treatment may be worthwhile.

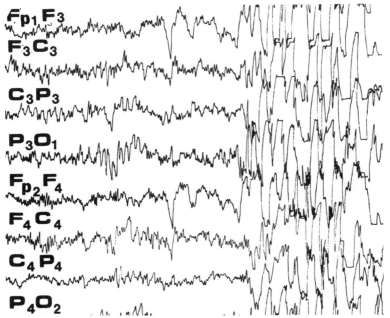

Figure 6-1. An EEG showing a burst of generalized spike-and-slow wave dysrhythmia. This pattern can be associated with absence seizures and may explain momentary staring and lapses of attention in children with ADHD and learning disorders.

The EEG can be helpful in the differentiation of epilepsy and daydreaming of the inattentive child with ADHD. The test is useful not only in diagnosis but also in treatment of learning and behavior disorders. Central nervous system stimulants and some antidepressants may precipitate seizures and should be used with caution in children with seizure activity in the EEG.

Attentional difficulties in children with some types of epilepsy are related to dysfunction in the right cerebral hemisphere and are associated with impaired visuospatial processing. Left hemisphere dysfunction causes language-related learning disabilities. The side of the epileptic EEG focus is linked to the type of learning deficit (Piccirilli M et al, 1994).

Q: Can behavior disorders represent a form of epilepsy?

A: Episodic hyperkinetic behavior may sometimes occur as a manifestation of epilepsy, but the diagnosis is often not clearly determined and "behavioral epilepsy" is controversial. A 4-year-old boy with benign partial epilepsy and hyperkinetic behavior between seizures is reported from Sapporo Medical University, Japan. Seizures consisted of a terrified expression, crouching, and rubbing his face on the floor. An EEG during a seizure in his sleep showed slow rhythms over the left hemisphere followed by depression of the voltage. Both the seizures and the hyperkinetic behavior responded to carbamazepine anticonvulsant therapy. The epilepsy was characterized as benign partial epilepsy with affective symptoms (Wakai S et al, 1994).

The association of an epileptiform EEG and a behavior disorder is sometimes considered to be coincidental (Okubo Y et al, 1994). However, if the behavioral symptoms are paroxysmal or appear in episodes, a trial of antiepileptic medication is justified.

HEADACHE DISORDERS AND ADHD

Q: How prevalent are the various forms of headache among school children with ADHD?

A: The main forms of headache among children are as follows: migraine, tension-type headache, post-traumatic headache, sinus related headache, and diet related headache. Headache can also be a symptom of brain tumor, and a manifestation of raised intracranial pressure. Stress at school and stimulant medication are headache precipitants, especially in children with ADHD.

In my own practice, a study of recurrent headaches diagnosed in 100 consecutive children found 42% were migrainous in type and 58% nonmigrainous. Of the migrainous types, 27% were classical migraine and 15% common migraine. Nonmigrainous headaches were of the tension type in 18%, tension associated with ADHD and learning disabilities in 21%, epilepsy equivalents in 18%, and in one the headaches were caused by an intracranial arachnoid cyst. Boys were affected in 60% and girls in 40% (Millichap JG, 1978).

Prevalence of migraine headaches in children has varied in different studies, depending on the age and sex of the children, and the definition of migraine. The average prevalence is 5%, or 1 in 20 school children.

In a random sample of the childhood population of the City of Aberdeen, Scotland, migraine was diagnosed by interview in 11%, more than twice the average prevalence quoted in previous pediatric studies (Abu-Arefeh I, Russell G, 1994). Tension headache occurred in 1%, and sinusitis in 0.2%. Boys suffered from migraine more frequently than girls under 12 years of age, and girls predominated over 12 years of age. Children with headache lost a mean of 8 days of school a year as compared to 3 days lost for control subjects.

In a population-based study of more than 1000 school children in Goteborg, Sweden, the prevalence of frequent headache increased with age and school grade, from 3% in second grade to 10% in third grade. The risk of frequent headache correlated with class size, increasing with larger classes. An increased prevalence of headache among girls in higher school grades was linked to possible hormonal changes and greater sensitivity to interpersonal conflicts and family stress (Carlsson J, 1996).

The prevalence of headache, including migraine, increased significantly between 1972 and 1992, in school age children living in an urban area of Finland. Migraine in 7-year-olds was recorded by school physicians at the time of routine medical examinations in 1.9% in 1974 and 5.7% in 1992. The highest increases occurred among children exposed to social instability and stress (Sillanpaa M, Anttila P, 1996). Similar increases in the prevalence of migraine were reported in the 1980s among adults in the United States.

Q: When is a headache a migraine?

A: The diagnosis of migraine as distinct from tension and other forms of headache is important in management and avoidance of migraine precipitating factors, such as dietary items.

Migraine is classified as 1) migraine without aura (common migraine), and 2) migraine with aura (classical migraine). Classical migraine occurs more commonly in adults than in children. Simple criteria required for the diagnosis of *common migraine* in children are as follows (any two of the four features):

1) Headache on one side of the head.

2) Headache of a pulsating quality.

3) Nausea associated with the headache.

4) Photophobia or phonophobia (light or noise intolerance) with headache.

If the above criteria are preceded within one hour by visual hallucinations (bright lights or figures) or sensations of numbness or tingling lasting 5 to 60 minutes, the headaches are diagnosed as *classical migraine* or migraine with aura (sensations).

A family history of migraine is a frequent finding that supports the diagnosis. Unlike tension headaches that often occur daily, migraine headaches recur at intervals of a week or usually longer. When symptoms are atypical, organic disease such as brain tumor must be ruled out.

Q: What are the indications for EEG and MRI or CT in children with headaches and ADHD?

A: An EEG or MRI is not indicated as a routine examination in children with recurrent headaches and ADHD. An EEG should be considered under the following conditions:

• Headaches in a child with a history of seizures or loss of consciousness.

• Episodes of weakness, unsteadiness, or numbness associated with the headache.

• Vomiting and/or drowsiness with the headache.

MRI or CT imaging is warranted in the following:

• Children with headaches associated with vomiting, especially those occurring on awakening in the morning.

• MRI is mandatory in patients with headaches and other signs of raised intracranial pressure that indicate a diagnosis of brain tumor or hemorrhage.

• Headaches and a focal abnormality in the EEG which might indicate a structural abnormality in the brain, such as arachnoid cyst.

Patients having abnormalities in the EEG or brain structural abnormalities on MRI may need special methods of management of headaches and ADHD.

The utility of EEG and MRI in children with headaches is reviewed in Progress in Pediatric Neurology III (Millichap JG, 1997). The risk of an adverse reaction to CT contrast medium or to heavy sedation necessary for MRI in young children must be weighed against the indications and potential benefits of the study.

Q: How should headaches with ADHD be treated?

A: If uncommon specific causes of headache such as intracranial tumor, seizures, or sinusitis have been excluded by history and examination, the emphasis in treatment is toward relief of stress and tensions at school or at home, modification in dosage or type of stimulant medication for ADHD, and investigation of possible hypersensitivity to food items. Intermittent pain relieving medications are usually effective for acute attacks of headache.

Family or individual counselling with a psychologist can uncover reasons for stress-related headache. Larger doses of methylphenidate or amphetamines may need to be reduced or omitted, and alternative treatments considered. Dietary items known to induce headaches in some individuals, such as chocolate, caffeine-containing sodas, hot dogs, aged cheeses, and dairy products, may need to be eliminated in sequence and for periods of up to 10 days. Relief of symptoms should be followed by a challenge with the offending food or drink, to determine the significance of the apparent sensitivity. Long-term drug treatment for migraine in children is rarely necessary or advisable, provided the headache precipitants are uncovered and managed effectively.

Q: How do children think about and deal with headaches?

A: Developmental issues related to headache management were investigated by psychologists at the University of South Alabama, Mobile, AL. A child's explanation of headache and description of the pain helps in understanding the cause and best approach to management. A shift from emphasizing external methods of control to acknowledging self-control of headache occurs with increasing age. Treatments incorporating self-regulation of stress factors, such as biofeedback training, depend on the development of a child's awareness of effects of external events on the headaches. Attention and emphasis by the family on headache-free days can be a strong treatment reinforcer in children, focusing less attention on the symptom (Marcon RA, Labbe EE, 1990). Adding a developmental perspective to psychological interventions in the management of childhood headache is likely to increase treatment effectiveness.

REFERENCES

Abu-Arefeh I, Russell G. Prevalence of headache and migraine in schoolchildren. BMJ 1994;309:765-769.

Baumgardner TL, Singer HS, Denckla MB et al. Corpus callosum morphology in children with Tourette syndrome and attention deficit hyperactivity disorder. Neurology 1996;47:477-482.

Caine ED et al. Tourette's syndrome in Monroe County school children. Neurology 1988;38:472-475.

Carlsson J. Prevalence of headache in schoolchildren: Relation to family and school factors. Acta Paediatr 1996;85:692-696.

Carter AS et al. A prospective longitudinal study of Gilles de la Tourette's syndrome. J Am Acad Child Adolesc Psychiatry 1994;33:377-385.

Chappell PB, Riddle MA et al. Guanfacine treatment of comorbid attention-deficit hyperactivity disorder and Tourette's syndrome. J Am Acad Child Adolesc Psychiatry 1995;34:1140-1146.

Eapen V, Moriarty J, Robertson MM. Stimulus induced behaviors in Tourette's syndrome. J Neurol Neurosurg Psychiatry 1994;57:853-855).

Eapen V et al. Sex of parent transmission effect in Tourette's syndrome: Evidence for earlier age at onset in maternally transmitted cases suggests a genomic imprinting effect. Neurology 1997;48:934-937.

Giedd JN, Rapoport JL et al. Case study: Acute basal ganglia enlargement and obsessive-compulsive symptoms in an adolescent boy. J am Acad Child Adolesc Psychiatry 1996;35:913-915.

Goodman & Gilman, The Pharmacological Basis of Therapeutics, 9th ed. New York, McGraw Hill, 1996.

Guttmann E et al (1927; In Wilson SAK. Neurology. Baltimore, Williams and Wilkins, 1955, p1924.

Kerbeshian J et al. Comorbid Tourette's disorder and bipolar disorder: an etiologic perspective. Am J Psychiatry 1995;152:1646-1651.

Kiesling LS et al. Antineuronal antibodies in movement disorders. Pediatrics 1993:92:39-43.

Kurlan R et al. Transient tic disorder and the spectrum of Tourette's syndrome. Arch Neurol 1988;45:1200-1201.

Lajonchere C et al. Historical review of Gilles de la Tourette syndrome. Arch Neurol 1996;53:567-574.

Lang A. Patient perception of tics and other movement disorders. Neurology 1991;41:223-228.

Lombroso PJ et al. Exacerbation of Gilles de la Tourette's syndrome associated with thermal stress: a family study. Neurology 1991;41:1984-1987.

Marcon RA, Labbe EE. Assessment and treatment of children's headaches from a developmental perspective. Headache 1990;30:586-592.

Millichap JG. Ed. Learning Disabilities and Related Disorders: Facts and Current Issues. Chicago, Year Book Med Publ, 1977.

Millichap JG. Recurrent headaches in 100 children. Electroencephalographic abnormalities and response to phenytoin (Dilantin). Child's Brain 1978;4:95-104.

Millichap JG. Ed. Progress in Pediatric Neurology II. Chicago, PNB Publishers, 1994;pp227-246.

Millichap JG. Ed. Progress in Pediatric Neurology III, Chicago, PNB Publishers, 1997;pp257-258.

Northram RS, Singer HS. Postencephalitic acquired Tourette-like syndrome in a child. Neurology 1991;41:592-593.

Okubo Y et al. Epileptiform EEG discharges in healthy children: Prevalence, emotional and behavioral correlates, and genetic influences. Epilepsia 1994;35:832-841.

Piccirilli M et al. Attention problems in epilepsy: Possible significance of the epileptogenic focus. Epilepsia 1994;35:1091-1096.

Schuerholz LJ et al. Learning disabilities in children with Tourette syndrome and ADHD. Neurology 1996;46:958-965.

Schwabe MJ, Konkol RJ. Menstrual cycle-related fluctuations of tics in Tourette syndrome. Pediatr Neurol 1992;8:43-46.

Sillanpaa M, Anttila P. Increasing prevalence of headache in 7-year-old schoolchildren. Headache 1996;36:466-470.

Singer HS, Denckla MB et al. Volumetric MRI changes in basal ganglia of children with Tourette's syndrome. Neurology 1993;43:950-956.

Spencer T, Biederman J et al. The relationship between tic disorders and Tourette's syndrome. J Am Acad Child Adolesc Psychiatry 1995;34:1133-1139.

Wakai S et al. Benign partial epilepsy with affective symptoms: Hyperkinetic behavior during interictal periods. Epilepsia 1994;35:810-812.

Wilson, SA Kinnear. Neurology 2nd ed. Baltimore, Williams and Wilkins, 1955.

CHAPTER 7

OPPOSITIONAL, CONDUCT AND OTHER ADHD COMORBID DISORDERS

Psychiatric disorders sometimes associated with ADHD include **oppositional defiant disorder, conduct disorder, mood disorders,** and **anxiety disorders,** including **obsessive compulsive disorder.** These are referred to as comorbid disorders. They complicate the management of ADHD, and if severe enough to impair school and social functioning, will require psychiatric or psychological intervention. For practical purposes, the following definitions are simplified from the DSM-IV diagnostic criteria.

Q: What is oppositional defiant disorder?

A: The criteria for the diagnosis of oppositional defiant disorder include at least five of the following, present for at least six months:

- Loses temper often
- Argues with adults
- Refuses to do chores
- Annoys other people
- Blames others
- Easily annoyed
- Often angry
- Often spiteful
- Swears frequently

Q: *How is a conduct disorder defined?*

A: A conduct disorder is significant if at least three of the following criteria have been present for at least six months:

- Steals
- Runs away from home
- Lies
- Sets fires
- Plays truant
- Breaks into someones house, building, or car
- Destroys others property
- Cruel to animals and/or people
- Sexually abusive
- Starts fights, with or without a weapon

Q: *How are mood disorders recognized?*

A: Mood disorders include manic and/or depressive episodes, bipolar disorders, cyclothymia, and dysthymia.

A *manic episode* consists of elevated or irritable mood sufficient to impair school and social functioning and associated with at least three of the following:

- Heightened self-esteem
- Sleeplessness
- Excessive talking
- Flight of ideas
- Distractibility
- Excessive goal directed activity
- Excessive spending and buying sprees

A *depressive episode* is recognized by at least five of the following symptoms, persisting for at least two weeks, and one consisting of either depressed mood or loss of interest in activities:

- Depressed mood
- Loss of interest in activities
- Loss or abnormal increase in weight
- Inability to sleep or excessive sleepiness
- Restless or sluggish
- Excessive fatigue
- Guilt feelings
- Inability to think or concentrate
- Thoughts of death or suicide

Bipolar disorders are manic, depressive, or both, with recurring manic or depressive episodes, not necessarily meeting the full criteria for diagnosis.

Cyclothymia is characterized by numerous hypomanic and depressed, but not major, episodes over one year or longer and never without some symptoms for more than two months at a time.

Dysthymia   is a depressed or irritable mood occurring daily, without major depression, for at least one year and manifested by at least two of the following:

- Poor or excessive appetite
- Loss of or excess sleep
- Loss of energy or fatigue
- Poor self-esteem
- Inability to focus and concentrate
- Feelings of hopelessness

Q: What are the anxiety disorders?

A: Anxiety disorders include panic disorder, phobias, obsessive compulsive disorder, post-traumatic stress disorder, and generalized anxiety disorder.

Panic disorders   are characterized by shortness of breath, dizziness, rapid heart rate, trembling, sweating, and choking. Mitral valve prolapse may be associated with these symptoms, and amphetamine or caffeine toxicity, or elevated thyroid levels can mimic the syndrome.

Phobias   include a fear of being alone in groups, in crowds, on bridges, and traveling alone (agoraphobia); and a fear of speaking in public or answering questions in class (social phobias). Children may have a fear of attending birthday parties or other group functions.

Obsessive compulsive disorder   consists of recurrent and persistent, unreasonable ideas and thoughts (obsessions), and repetitive, purposeful, excessive behaviors in response to obsessions (compulsions). Examples of compulsive behavior include repetitive touching of objects and washing of hands.

Post-traumatic stress disorder is an abnormal reaction to a distressing event, characterized by recurring distressing recollections or dreams related to the trauma, avoidance of activities related to the trauma, sleep disturbance, irritability, and inability to concentrate on school work.

Generalized anxiety disorder consists of an abnormal degree of anxiety and worry about school grades and social interaction with peers. Symptoms include trembling, restlessness, palpitations, sweating, dizziness, difficulty concentrating, and irritability. Caffeine intoxication or excess thyroid can mimic the symptoms of anxiety disorder.

Q: How prevalent are these psychiatric disorders among children with ADHD?

A: Children with ADHD complicated by severe mood disorders and anxiety disorders are likely to be referred primarily to the child psychiatrist or psychologist. Those with mild to moderate oppositional defiant and conduct disorders are often seen initially by the pediatrician and pediatric neurologist. Estimates of prevalence of these comorbid disorders are dependent on the specialty of the treating physician, and higher rates of occurrence might be expected among children referred to psychiatric clinics and psychologists. The majority of research studies involving ADHD children with comorbid psychiatric disorders have been conducted in psychiatry departments of major universities and medical centers. Lower prevalence rates might be expected among children treated in child neurology clinics.

Q: What is the relation between oppositional defiant and conduct disorders and ADHD?

A: Oppositional defiant disorder (ODD) is a more common ADHD-comorbid problem than conduct disorder (CD). The majority of children with ADHD do not have CD. Those who have CD develop the disorder before age 12 years, and almost always show symptoms of ODD for several years previously.

ODD children with CD, and those without, have different outcomes. CD with ADHD is associated with a higher frequency of substance abuse in adolescence, and higher incidence of anxiety and mood disorders.

The link between oppositional defiant disorder (ODD), conduct disorder (CD), and ADHD was evaluated at the Pediatric Psychiatric Service, Massachusetts General Hospital, Boston (Biederman J et al, 1996). The findings were as follows:

• Of 140 children with ADHD, 65% had comorbid ODD and 22% had CD at initial examination.

• Of ODD children, 32% had comorbid CD.

• Children with CD also had ODD that preceded CD by several years.

• Children with both ODD and CD had more severe symptoms of ODD, more psychiatric disorders, including more bipolar disorder, and more abnormal behavior scores compared to ADHD children without comorbidity.

Neurological soft signs have been found to correlate with the occurrence of symptoms of ODD and

CD, as well as anxiety, phobias, depression or dysthmia. In a study of 56 high-risk boys, 7 to 10 years old, at the New York State Psychiatric Institute, NY (Pine DS et al, 1997), the demonstration of soft signs at neurological examination was a risk factor for childhood onset psychiatric symptoms, as well as ADHD.

Q: What factors predispose to conduct disorders in children with ADHD?

A: ADHD and learning disabilities contribute to conduct disorders, but the main cause is linked to harsh, inconsistent parenting. Studies at Queens College, Flushing, NY (Halperin JM et al, 1997), and the Institute of Psychiatry, London (Scott S, 1998), both demonstrated a relation between parent aggressive behavior and aggression in the children, especially boys. Aggressive behavior occurred in 10% of children in an urban population, and the majority of juvenile delinquents had conduct disorders by age 7 years. Reduced serotonergic function, a neurochemical mechanism, was associated with aggression in the NY study.

Q: What is the influence of an adverse family environment on ADHD and comorbid disorders?

A: Adverse family environments, chronic parental conflicts, and psychiatric illness affecting the mother influence the outcome of ADHD and the response to treatment. In a study of 140 ADHD children at the Massachusetts General Hospital, Biederman and his associates (1995) found increased levels of environmental adversity among ADHD compared to control subjects. Parental conflict and exposure to mothers with psychiatric illness were especially prevalent. Surprisingly, the risk of developing comorbid conduct disorder, depression or anxiety was not influenced by environmental adverse factors.

In a study of psychiatric and developmental disorders in families of children with ADHD, researchers at the University of Chicago (Roizen NJ et al, 1996) found that children with ADHD were more likely to have a parent affected by alcoholism, other drug abuse, depression, delinquency, learning disabilities, and/or ADHD. Children with a family history of psychiatric disorders should be screened for ADHD. Psychosocial intervention is recommended for families affected.

Q: Can conduct disorders in children if untreated lead to adult criminality?

A: ADHD children with conduct disorders are at an increased risk for criminal behavior and arrest in adolescence and in adulthood, according to a study in the Division of Child Psychiatry, Oregon Health Sciences University, Portland, OR (Satterfield JH, Schell A, 1997). Childhood severe conduct disorders and adolescent antisocial behavior, if not treated by early psychosocial intervention, may be predictors of later arrest for criminality.

In some studies, hyperactive children are five times more likely to develop conduct disorders and a subsequent increased rate of criminality than average.

Stealing from other children, and telling lies to get out of trouble are conduct problems that appear minor but may lead to more serious antisocial behavior in adolescence, unless treated by early psychological intervention.

Q: What is the relation of mood and anxiety disorders to ADHD?

A: Psychiatrists frequently find a cause and effect relationship between the symptoms of ADHD and anxiety or depression (Silver LB, 1992). In contrast, neurologists favor an organic biological etiology for ADHD and regard anxiety or mood disorders as secondary symptoms, sometimes precipitated by stimulant treatment (Millichap JG, 1997). A depressive reaction induced by methylphenidate occurs particularly with larger doses and in children with a genetic vulnerability to mood disorders (Weinberg WA et al, 1997).

A familial relationship between ADHD and bipolar disorder (BPD) was examined in 140 children with ADHD and BPD and their first degree relatives at the Pediatric Psychopharmacology Unit, Massachusetts General Hospital, Boston (Faraone SV et al, 1997). The risk of BPD among relatives was increased 5-fold if the child with ADHD also suffered from BPD. The comorbid presentation of ADHD and BPD appeared to represent a distinct subtype of ADHD, predominantly affecting boys, and with a high familial risk of ADHD, BPD, and major depression. However, this subtype was rare, occurring in only 5% of children with ADHD. The findings did not support a theory of depression as a cause of ADHD.

Pediatric neurologists are frequently faced with the

differentiation of organic and psychiatric causes for behavioral and mood disorders complicated by complaints of hyperactivity, distractibility and impulsivity. The recognition of early onset mood disorders should permit prompt withdrawal or dose reduction of stimulant therapy and referral to colleagues specializing in child psychology and psychiatry when appropriate.

An association between adolescent mania and ADHD is reported from the Department of Psychiatry, University of Cincinnati, Ohio (West SA et al, 1995). Of 14 adolescent bipolar patients admitted to hospital for the treatment of acute mania or hypomania, 8 (57%) met the DSM criteria for a diagnosis of ADHD. Patients with ADHD had higher scores on a Mania Rating Scale than those with bipolar disorder alone.

Clinical symptoms and outcome of childhood-onset dysthymic disorder (DD) were compared with major depressive disorder (MDD) in a 3- to 12-year study of two groups of school-age patients treated at the Psychiatric Departments of the Universities of Pittsburgh, and California at San Diego, and Harvard University (Kovacs M et al, 1994). Dysthymic disorder had an earlier age of onset than MDD, similar symptoms of feeling unloved, irritability and anger, but lower frequencies of guilt feelings, impaired concentration, loss of appetite, insomnia, and fatigue. Risk of MDD and bipolar disorder was increased in dysthymic patients.

Oppositional defiant and conduct disorders were present more often in a dysthymic group of patients than in those with major depression, treated as in-patients in a child psychiatry unit at State University of New York at Stony Brook (Ferro T et al, 1994).

Children with the combined subtype of ADHD (inattentive and hyperactive-impulsive) showed the greatest psychiatric impairments compared to other subtypes in a study at the Pediatric Psycho-pharmacology Unit, Massachusetts General Hospital, Boston (Faraone SV et al, 1998). Hyperactive-impulsive patients were not different from controls on measures of depression, social functioning, IQ, and academic achievement.

Q: Is ADHD a risk factor for drug abuse disorders in adolescents?

A: Adolescents with or without ADHD have a similar risk of alcohol or drug abuse disorders (*psychoactive substance use disorders*). Drug abuse occurred in 15% of 140 ADHD adolescents and with the same frequency in 120 normal control subjects. ADHD alone does not predispose to drug abuse during adolescence. Patients and controls were followed for four years at the Department of Psychiatry, Massachusetts General Hospital, Boston (Biederman J et al, 1997).

The risk of alcohol and drug abuse was increased in patients with a history of conduct or bipolar disorders, but not in those with oppositional defiant disorder, major depression or anxiety. Oppositional defiant disorder, uncomplicated by conduct disorder, did not predict drug abuse.

Q: Are adults with ADHD more susceptible to drug abuse than adolescents?

A: Studies show that adults with ADHD are more susceptible to drug abuse than adolescents. A sharp increase in drug abuse can be expected in adolescent

ADHD subjects as they become adults, especially if they have not previously received treatment for ADHD.

In a study of comorbid ADHD and substance abuse among adolescents and adults, reported from the Veteran's Affairs Medical Center, West Haven, CT, substance use and abuse were related to attempts to self-medicate symptoms of ADHD, especially in previously untreated adolescents. Prescribed medical treatment for ADHD was found to decrease drug craving in adults with comorbid ADHD and drug abuse and to improve functioning (Horner BR, Scheibe KE, 1997).

Adult psychiatric status of hyperactive boys grown up, examined at the Long Island Jewish Medical Center, and NY State Psychiatric Institute, found that antisocial personality disorder and nonalcohol substance abuse occurred in 12%, compared to 3% of controls (Mannuzza S et al, 1998). Shaffer D, also from the NY State Psychiatric Institute, reported in 1994 that substance abuse disorder is commonly associated with a diagnosis of ADHD in adults.

Biederman J et al (1995), at the Massachusetts General Hospital, found that childhood onset ADHD persisting in adults carried a 40% risk of substance abuse disorders, most commonly marijuana. No differences in the preferred drugs of abuse between ADHD adults and normal control subjects were observed. A concern of parents that ADHD children treated with methylphenidate may later show an increased tendency to abuse stimulant drugs was not supported.

Risk factors for persistence of ADHD into adolescence included a genetic familial tendency to ADHD, psychosocial adversity and exposure to parental conflict, and comorbidity with conduct, mood and anxiety disorders. Clearly, psychosocial intervention and appropriate medication at an early age are important in prevention of substance abuse disorders in adults with pervasive ADHD.

Q: Is ADHD a risk factor for early cigarette smoking in children and adolescents?

A: ADHD, particularly when associated with conduct disorders, is a significant risk factor for early cigarette smoking in children and adolescents. This was the conclusion of a study at the Massachusetts General Hospital, Boston (Milberger S et al, 1997). Effects of early treatment of ADHD on the susceptibility to cigarette smoking would be of interest.

Q: Is obsessive compulsive disorder an emotional or organic neurologic disorder?

A: Generally classified as an anxiety neurosis, obsessive compulsive disorder (OCD) has recently been associated with structural abnormalities in the basal ganglia, an area of the brain involved with involuntary movements. MRI scans of 19 children, aged 7 to 18 years, with recent onset OCD showed significantly reduced volumes of the striatal basal ganglia structures, in a study at the Western Psychiatric Institute, University of Pittsburgh, PA (Rosenberg DR et al, 1997). Reduced striatal volume was inversely correlated with the severity of OCD symptoms; the smaller the basal ganglia, the more severe the symptoms. These findings are the opposite of those suggested by a previous report involving a child with acute symptoms of OCD.

An acute enlargement of the basal ganglia was correlated with an acute exacerbation of obsessive-compulsive disorder (OCD) and tics in a 12-year-old boy monitored by MRI at the National Institute of Mental Health, Bethesda, MD (Giedd JN et al, 1996). The symptoms followed a streptococcal throat infection, and treatment resulted in shrinkage in size of the basal ganglia and reduction in symptoms of OCD and tics.

Structural changes in the brain correlating with severity of symptoms support an organic basis for OCD, but further and more definitive studies are indicated. A trial of antibiotics may be beneficial in children whose symptoms of OCD and tics are associated with recent streptococcal infection and persistently elevated serum antistreptolysin titers.

Q: What is Asperger's syndrome and can it mimic ADHD?

A: Asperger's syndrome (AS), first described as "autistic psychopathy" by an Austrian psychiatrist, Hans Asperger in 1944, includes language delays, poor social skills, peculiar interests and motor clumsiness. AS is classified as a subgroup of the autistic spectrum disorders.

The characteristic diagnostic criteria of AS include a formal concrete way of thinking, and an inability to identify and understand human emotions and relationships. Communication difficulties range from stilted speech to almost robotic manner. Abnormal preoccupations include toy cars, insects, fungi, poisons, violence to babies, ritualistic drawings and excessive orderliness (Perkins M, Wolkind SN, 1991; Tuchman RF, 1991). Asperger's syndrome may overlap or occur concurrently with Tourette syndrome (Nass R, Gutman R, 1997), pervasive developmental disorder, and attention deficit disorder.

Symptoms that might be confused with ADHD are related to learning disorders, despite average or superior intelligence, especially areas involving language, spelling, reading and visual memory. The neurologic examination reveals motor incoordination and nonspecific EEG abnormalities, indicative of minimal brain dysfunction. A genetic factor is suspected but no specific organic pathology has been identified.

The manifestations of Asperger's syndrome that clearly distinguish this psychiatric disorder from ADHD are the peculiar personality and communication difficulties resembling an autistic illness. Asperger's syndrome should be considered in children of high verbal intelligence who do poorly in school, both academically and socially, and who exhibit speech and language disorders, tics, motor clumsiness, and stereotyped movements such as repetitive hand flapping.

Multiple biological causes for autism and autistic-like disorders were uncovered in a study of 52 affected children examined neurologically at the University of Goteborg, Sweden (Steffenburg S, 1991). The EEG was abnormal in 50% and the CT scan showed structural brain abnormalities in 25%.

The pediatric neurology examination is important in children with autistic-like symptoms, and EEG and CT may be indicated in selected patients. Biological disorders may be uncovered in children with symptoms thought to be primarily psychiatric and emotionally based (Millichap JG, 1994).

REFERENCES

Biederman J et al. Impact of adversity on functioning and comorbidity in children with attention-deficit hyperactivity disorder. J Am Acad Child Adolesc Psychiatry 1995;34:1495-1503.

Biederman J et al. Psychoactive substance use disorders in adults with attention deficit hyperactivity disorder (ADHD): effects of ADHD and comorbidity. Am J Psychiatry 1995;152:1652-1658.

Biederman J et al. Predictors of persistence and remission of ADHD into adolescence: results from a four-year prospective follow-up study. J Am Acad Child Adolesc Psychiatry 1996;35:343-351.

Biederman J et al. Is childhood oppositional defiant disorder a precursor to adolescent conduct disorder? Findings from a four-year follow-up study of children with ADHD. J Am Acad Child Adolesc Psychiatry 1996;35:1193-1204.

Biederman J et al. Is ADHD a risk factor for psychoactive substance use disorders? Findings from a four-year prospective follow-up study. J Am Acad Child Adolesc Psychiatry 1997;36:21-29.

Faraone SV et al. Attention-deficit hyperactivity disorder with bipolar disorder: a familial subtype? J Am Acad Child Adolesc Psychiatry 1997;36:1378-1387.

Faraone SV et al. Psychiatric, neuropsychological, and psychosocial features of DSM-IV subtypes of ADHD. J Am Acad Child Adolesc Psychiatry 1998;37:185-193.

Ferro T et al. Depressive disorders: Distinctions in children. J Am Acad Child Adolesc Psychiatry 1994;33:664-670.

Giedd JN, et al. Case study: Acute basal ganglia enlargement and obsessive-compulsive symptoms in an adolescent boy. J Am Acad Child Adolesc Psychiatry 1996;35:913-915.

Horner BR, Scheibe KE. Prevalence and implications of attention-deficit hyperactivity disorder among adolescents in treatment for substance abuse. J Am Acad Child Adolesc Psychiatry 1997;36:30-36.

Kovacs M et al. Childhood-onset dysthymic disorder. Clinical features and prospective naturalistic outcome. Arch Gen Psychiatry 1994;51:365-374.

Mannuzza S et al. Adult psychiatric status of hyperactive boys grown up. Am J Psychiatry 1998;155:493-498.

Milberger S et al. ADHD is associated with early initiation of cigarette smoking in children and adolescents. J Am Acad Child Adolesc Psychiatry 1997;36:37-44.

Millichap JG. Progress in Pediatric Neurology II. Chicago, PNB Publishers, 1994.

Millichap JG. Progress in Pediatric Neurology III. Chicago, PNB Publishers, 1997.

Nass R, Gutman R. Boys with Asperger's disorder, exceptional verbal intelligence, tics, and clumsiness. Dev Med Child Neurol 1997;39:691-695.

Perkins M, Wolkind SN. Asperger's syndrome: who is being abused? Arch Dis Child 1991;66:693-695.

Pine DS et al. Neurological soft signs: one-year stability and relationship to psychiatric symptoms in boys. J Am Acad Child Adolesc Psychiatry 1997;36:1579-1586.

Roizen NJ et al. Psychiatric and developmental disorders in families of children with ADHD. Arch Pediatr Adolesc Med 1996;150:203-208.

Rosenberg DR et al. Frontostriatal measurement in treatment-naive children with obsessive-compulsive disorder. Arch Gen Psychiatry 1997;54:824-830.

Satterfield JH, Schell A. A prospective study of hyperactive
    boys with conduct problems and normal boys: adolescent
    and adult criminality. J Am Acad Child Adolesc Psychiatry
    1997;36:1726-1735.

Scott S. Conduct disorder in children in the UK. BMJ
    1998;316:202-206.

Silver LB. Attention-Deficit Hyperactivity Disorder. A Clinical
    Guide to Diagnosis and Treatment. Washington, DC,
    American Psychiatric Press, 1992.

Steffenburg S. Neuropsychiatric assessment of children with
    autism: a population-based study. Dev Med Child Neurol
    1991;33:495-511.

Tuchman RF. Autism: delineating the spectrum. Int Pediatr
    1991;6:161-169.

Weinberg WA et al. Depressive reaction induced by
    methylphenidate. J Pediatr 1997;130:665-669.

West SA et al. ADHD and adolescent mania. Am J Psychiatry
    1995;152:271-273.

CHAPTER **8**

METHODS OF MANAGEMENT OF ADHD

Several methods and disciplines are involved in the management of the child with ADHD. These include participation of the parents, teachers, psychologist and physicians. The parents, and especially the mother, may be the first to draw attention to the problem, even in the preschool years. The teacher generally reports concerns about a child's inattention, hyperactivity and impulsive behavior in kindergarten or first grade. The psychologist becomes involved either on referral from the teacher or after consultation with the physician. The pediatrician, pediatric neurologist or child psychiatrist is usually consulted to confirm the diagnosis and to supervise the management of medical therapy.

Stimulant medications may have the most

remarkable and prompt benefical effects in the treatment of ADHD, but without family counseling, behavior modification and remedial education, drugs alone will have only a partial and sometimes transitory value. The physician is in the ideal position to ensure that this so-called "multimodal" approach to the management of ADHD is followed, since the patient and parents will be seen at regular intervals for monitoring of effects and renewal of prescriptions. Reports from teachers, psychologist and counselor should be made available to the physician at follow-up examinations.

Q: What are the principal forms of therapy of ADHD?

A: A single approach to the management of ADHD is never completely satisfactory, despite the dramatic early benefits of stimulant therapy. In addition to medications which are discussed more fully in the next chapter, important therapeutic regimens include the following:

- Psychological and psychosocial intervention.
- Parent and family counseling.
- Behavior modification and/or child counseling.
- Remedial education and learning accommodations

The optimal order of introduction of these various methods of management is somewhat controversial. Some psychologists favor initial psychosocial intervention and behavior modification management, whereas physicians prefer to introduce medication early as an essential aid to education and academic success.

Q: What are the roles of the psychologist and psychiatrist in the management of the child with ADHD?

A: The psychologist provides testing, diagnosis and/or counseling in group or individual sessions, and advises and monitors but does not generally prescribe medications. The psychiatrist diagnoses and treats with medications and psychotherapy. Some university based psychiatrists are psychopharmacologists, specializing in the research and trials of medications for ADHD and comorbid disorders.

Psychologists specialize as educational or clinical psychologists, providing testing and/or therapy. Some are trained to provide both types of services. A parent may consult a psychologist about symptoms of ADHD or a learning problem as a first resort or on the advice of the physician or teacher. At some point, a child who is having learning or behavioral problems will need the services of a psychologist. These may be provided through the school or mental health system or privately. The psychological effects of a handicapped child on family functioning and methods of counselling and training for families of children with ADHD, including peer relationships, are described by Barkley RA (1990, 1997) and Millichap MG (1984).

Q: How can the pediatric neurologist help the parents to understand and deal with the problem of ADHD?

A: Since the medical evidence supports a neurobiological or organic basis for ADHD, the major responsibility for the problem has been shifted from the parents to the child's brain and a neurochemical or structural brain deficit. The claim by sociologists and others that ADHD represents a "deviant behavior," largely under the control of the child and parent-child relationship, has been discounted by neurological research. The "medicalization" of ADHD and its treatment as an "illness" have been justified by the results of scientific studies.

The pediatric neurologist explains the factors known to underly the symptoms of ADHD, and orders tests to rule out specific causes as appropriate. While the physician is responsible for the diagnosis and medical management, the parents need to understand the influence of child-family interaction and remedial education on the success of treatment interventions. The parents have an equal responsibility to become educated in their role in the management of the child in the home. Parental conflict and environmental family adversity will exacerbate the symptoms of ADHD and diminish the effectiveness of medical treatment.

Q: What are some useful tips for parents and their role in management of ADHD?

A: To live with a hyperactive child demands patience and understanding from parents, siblings and neighbors. The following suggestions for parents may be found helpful:
  • Avoid repetition of "no" and "don't."
  • Use praise whenever appropriate and emphasize

successful activities to build self-confidence and self-esteem.

• Find an academic or sports interest that motivates a child and encourage and support it.

• Speak quietly and slowly.

• Present tasks or errands one at a time.

• Use written or picture cues to reinforce verbal requests or explanations.

• Encourage a structured, calm routine for homework, meal-times, playtime and bedtime.

• Avoid formal meals in restaurants if they lead to disruption and argument.

• Encourage less boisterous playmates and avoid noisy activities.

• Obtain the help of a family counselor or psychologist, especially if the ADHD is complicated by oppositional defiant or conduct disorder.

Of all these parental interventions, perhaps the emphasis on motivation is the most important.

Q: Why are motivational techniques emphasized in parent counseling and training sessions?

A: Parents often ask why their child can focus on an activity such as Nintendo or a favorite television program while exhibiting distractibility and inattentiveness in school. The answer is related to the nature of attention and the influence of environmental demands and distractions.

The learning process has been classified in four categories: 1) goal-awareness, 2) vigilance, 3) selectivity, and 4) tenacity. The child with ADHD is usually hypervigilant, but has deficits in selection and sustaining attention (Rosenberger PB, 1991). The discrimination of essential from unessential stimuli is impaired. Attention can be redirected by situational demands and goal-awareness or motivation.

Parents can encourage the child to pursue appropriate interests by finding motivational activities and providing support and praise. Biographies of famous people who have overcome adversity to succeed in their chosen field of endeavor are excellent motivational tools.

Winston Spencer Churchill, who saved England from the tyranny of Hitler's Germany by his superior leadership and oratory, and later wrote a best-selling History of the British Empire, had symptoms of ADHD, a speech impediment and learning disability as a child (Churchill WS, 1930). In his autobiography, My Early Life, Churchill wrote: "I was on the whole considerably discouraged by my school days." "It is not pleasant to feel oneself so completely outclassed and left behind at the very beginning of the race." He was surprised on leaving school to hear his teacher predict, "with a confidence for which I could see no foundation, that I should be able to make my way all right." "I have always been very grateful to him for this remark."

A simple word of praise or note of confidence from a teacher makes its mark for life in a child with academic problems. Churchill did indeed make his way alright. He became Prime Minister of Great Britain and a World leader. Like Churchill, several famous people have been reported to suffer from learning disabilities during childhood. Thomas Edison, Albert Einstein, President Woodrow Wilson, and Governor Nelson

Rockefeller are among those listed as dyslexic, yet their names are indelibly written in the papers of history.

Nancy Millichap, in her book on Dyslexia (1986), refers to articles on the childhood of Thomas Edison and other historical figures. Thomas Edison, inventor, was diagnosed as mentally ill by his teacher, his father thought he was stupid, he never learned to spell, and up to the time of his manhood his grammar was appalling. Albert Einstein, physicist and Nobel prize winner, did not talk until he was four nor read until nine. He was considered backward by his teachers and his father. Woodrow Wilson, President of the United States, did not learn his letters until he was nine or learn to read until he was eleven. Nelson A. Rockefeller, the former governor of New York State and vice-president of the United States, in an article writen in the TV Guide, 1976, entitled "Don't Accept Anyone's Verdict That You are Lazy, Stupid, or Retarded," recalled his difficulties as a dyslexic boy before there were special schools and teachers for reading-disabled children. Nowadays, with our current understanding of dyslexia and other learning disabilities, the burden of a child's academic problems should be lighter and prospects brighter.

Q: What should the child with ADHD be told about the problem and the management?

A: The physician, parent and teacher each has a role in counseling the child with ADHD. Specialized psychological or psychiatric counseling is required in patients with behavior, mood or anxiety disorders, resistant to more simple measures. Behavior modification therapy employing rewards may be helpful as an adjunct to medical treatment.

The physician explains the nature of the disorder and purpose of medications. Methylphenidate (Ritalin®) is recommended as an aid to education, to help focus and lessen distractibility, not primarily to modify behavior. Although a practice debated by some, medicines may be omitted at weekends and on vacations, unless the child is engaged in a learning situation.

Parents should praise success, ignore failure, and avoid excessive or harsh criticism, but tolerance should be tempered with appropriate and consistent discipline. Teachers, with the help of the psychologist, explain the nature and reasons for the learning problem, emphasizing the strengths and showing how weaknesses may be corrected by training. A positive attitude of parents, teachers, and all professionals is the key to success.

Q: What is behavior modification therapy and how successful is it?

A: Behavior modification is a systematic form of environmental structuring, based on the hypothesis that behavior is governed by either pleasurable or denied gratification. It is assumed that a child will modify behavior to obtain rewards and to avoid restrictions, denials or reprimands.

A system of rewards, denials or reprimands is established and explained fully to the child and all members of the family. Both parents in the home and teachers in the classroom should be involved. Good or desirable behavior is rewarded and positively reinforced, and bad or undesirable behavior is negatively reinforced. Positive reinforcements are usually preferred and emphasized although immediate reprimands may be necessary as a more intense behavioral intervention. Tokens used as positive reinforcement are given to the child and exchanged for goods or services according to a schedule of rates and values. Time outs in a quiet room and denial or restriction of television viewing time are examples of negative reinforcements and the consequences of unacceptable behavior.

Classroom reinforcers include individualized attention, immediate and frequent praise for good work, and responsibility and rewards for special tasks. Reprimands, unlike token rewards, can be readily implemented by the teacher, and immediate reprimands are superior to those delayed. An Emory University study of ADHD children's responses to behavioral intervention alone and in combination with stimulant medication showed that immediate classroom teacher reprimands can achieve results comparable to those of stimulants. However, such behavioral interventions are labor intensive and not accessible to most children with ADHD. Furthermore, for some children medication will obviate the need for intensive behavioral intervention (Abramowitz AJ, Dulcan MK et al, 1992).

Behavior modification requires time, patience and some compulsiveness on the part of the parents, teachers and therapists, if the system is to be applied uniformly and consistently over an extended period. The detailed explanations necessary are usually outside the scope of most physicians in practice. Parents interested in the method should obtain professional assistance through the local community mental health center or a private consulting psychologist or psychiatrist.

In practice, behavior modification alone is rarely successful, but in combination with medication it can be of value. In children with ADHD complicated by ODD or CD, individual counseling with a psychologist or social worker is usually required.

Q: What is the role of the teacher and school system in the management of ADHD?

A: The teacher is often the first person to recognize a child's inattention, hyperactivity and impulsiveness, and to suspect a diagnosis of ADHD. After discussion with the parents, the teacher may complete ADHD and behavioral questionnaires, such as the Conner, McCarney, or Quay and Peterson Rating Scales. On the basis of a child's inability to function satisfactorily in the normal classroom and the results of the questionnaires, further testing by a school psychologist or learning disability teacher may be implemented. A consultation with the child's pediatrician or with a pediatric neurologist will be suggested.

The appropriate accommodations in class placement and school curriculum should be made after parent-teacher conferences are completed. Learning disabilities uncovered by psychological tests should be remedied by special methods of education. The educational rights for children with ADD are protected by law.

Q: What are the Federal Laws relating to educational rights of children with ADHD?

A: Two federal laws guarantee appropriate education for children with ADHD enrolled in public schools or private schools receiving federal funds. These are the *Individuals with Disabilities Act (IDEA)* and *Section 504 of the Rehabilitation Act of 1973.* The Department of Education, in a "Policy Clarification Memorandum," dated September 16, 1991, stated that students with ADD may be eligible for special education and related services under Part B of the IDEA, solely on the basis of their ADD when it significantly impairs educational performance or learning.

As with other disabilities included under the IDEA, it must be established that the ADD has significant negative impact on a child's educational performance. A multidisciplinary team evaluation may be required to determine whether special education and/or related services are needed.

While the IDEA requires a child with ADD to have a learning problem for eligibility for special services, Section 504 covers children with behavior problems such as hyperactivity, not complicated by learning disabilities.

The Americans with Disabilities Act (ADA), 1990, provides additional legal requirements that cover children with ADD attending public schools and nonreligious private schools. A local CHADD (Children and Adults with Attention Deficit Disorders) chapter will provide parents with information if help is needed in obtaining special educational services.

Q: What are some of the classroom accommodations suggested for children with ADHD and learning disorders?

A: The Federal Government Department of Education suggests classroom accommodations which include the following examples:
- Structured learning environment.
- Individualized homework assignments.
- Written as well as verbal instructions.
- Untimed tests.
- Access to tape recorders and computers.
- Behavior modification techniques.

If remedial education and accommodations are advised by the psychologist and physician, the parent should meet with the teacher in order to discuss and implement the recommended changes in a child's curriculum. The parent is usually involved in this "individual educational plan."

Q: What types of special education placements are available for children with ADHD in public schools?

A: The various special education programs are graded according to the severity and type of the child's learning and/or behavior disorder, from mild to severe, as follows:
- Regular classroom plus part-time tutoring,
- Regular classroom plus part-time resource room, 1/2 - 2 hours daily.
- Part-time learning disability class plus resource

room and mainstreaming or integration into regular class for certain subjects.

- Full-time learning disability (LD) or behavior disorder (BD) class.
- Full-time "educable mentally handicapped" class (intended for children with an IQ of 60-80 and not classified as ADHD or LD).

The advantages of the resource room and the learning disability class are the small size, which allows for more individual attention, and staffing by teachers with special qualifications in the field of learning disorders. The disadvantage of such classes is the stigma of labeling and segregating the child from peers at an early age. However, if the purpose is explained to the child individually and to the class and parents, the special education is soon accepted when academic successes result.

Q: What are some of the professional support services available in public schools?

A: Specialized support services made available to children with ADHD attending public schools include the following:

- *School psychologist.* The psychologist is called upon to perform *individual* intelligence, perception, and reading tests if a child is thought to have a learning problem, and to evaluate social-emotional factors underlying behavior disorders. The *psychological evaluation* administered individually is different from the *achievement tests* (Iowa, Stanford, or California) which are administered to a group by the classroom or learning disability teacher at more frequent intervals. Parents are often confused about the functions and tests performed by the psychologist and the LD teacher.

• *Social worker.* The school social worker may provide counseling services for children with behavioral problems, and emotional support and reassurance for those dealing with issues such as divorce or peer pressures.

• *School nurse.* The school nurse often takes the responsibility for handing out medications at lunchtime, for reporting any side effects, and supervises records of required immunizations, and vision and hearing tests.

• *Remedial reading teacher.* Children with dyslexia or lesser degrees of reading difficulty can be referred to the reading specialist for individual or group instruction and training.

• *Speech pathologist.* Speech and language evaluations are performed by the school if a child's understanding and/or expressive language abilities are delayed. The speech pathologist also provides therapy individually or in groups.

• *School guidance counselor.* Guidance counselors are available particularly in high schools. They assist students with selection of classes, careers, and colleges. In lower grades a guidance counselor may help with tutors and decisions regarding grade placement or special schools.

• *Occupational therapist.* Occupational therapy (OT) sessions are sometimes advised for children with ADHD who have incoordination of motor movement and are described as clumsy. OT will often help in facilitating gross coordination, permitting children to participate in group physical activities.

Q: When are private or therapeutic schools indicated for children with ADHD?

A: Private educational facilities for children with ADHD are either day schools or boarding schools. The private day school or therapeutic school may be essential when the public school district is unable to provide appropriate special educational services. The boarding school may be the ideal placement for the child who requires special services in a well-structured environment on a 24-hour basis.

Children with both learning and language disorders may not show the expected rate of progress in regular public school placements, and may require more intensive and individualized teaching programs. The small teacher-pupil ratio in private schools is an advantage, but the fees necessary to provide this optimal placement are often prohibitive.

Q: What is the role of the tutor in the education of the child with ADHD?

A: Individual tutoring is the most flexible and least conspicuous method of providing special education. In addition to supplementing school instruction, the experienced tutor will often assume the role of counselor and advisor, bolstering self-confidence and allaying a child's anxieties about school performance. When a tutor is recommended, the choice should be made in consultation with the regular classroom teacher if possible. This allows continuity between the work in the classroom and homework.

Q: What are some of the resource groups and associations a parent may turn to for information on ADHD and learning disabilities?

A: A number of national and local resource groups provide information on ADHD for parents on request. The web site address for ADHD is as follows:

http://www.healthguide.com/adhd/

CHADD, the organization for Children and Adults with Attention Deficit Disorders, provides information and support for parents, including suggestions on parent training, medical management, and educational rights for children with ADD. They also provide information for teachers, and a review of controversial alternative treatments. Each local chapter has regular evening meetings, and frequent guest speakers who are experts in various aspects of ADHD.

CHADD, Children and Adults with Attention Deficit Disorders, national office address:
CHADD
499 NW 70th Ave, Suite 308
Plantation, FL 33317
Tel: 954-587-3700; Fax: 954-587-4599
Web site: http://www.chadd.org/

LDAA, the Learning Disabilities Association of America, arranges educational symposia on ADHD and learning disabilities, with invited speakers and research presentations. They also publish camp and college directories suited to young people with LD. Their address is as follows:

LDAA
4156 Library Road
Pittsburgh, PA 15234
Tel: 412-341-8077; Fax: 412-344-0224
Web site: http://www.ldanatl.org/

ADDA, National Attention Deficit Disorder Association:
P.O. Box 972, Mentor, OH 44606
Tel: 440-350-9595; Fax: 440-350-0223
Web site: http://www.add.org/
e-mail: Natl ADDA @ aol.com

National Center for Learning Disabilities
381 Park Avenue South, Suite 1401
New York, NY 10016
Tel: 212-545-7510; Fax: 212-545-9665

ORTON DYSLEXIA SOCIETY provides information on the study, treatment, and prevention of dyslexia. The society publishes a journal, Annals of Dyslexia, devoted to the history, research, and classroom perspectives of dyslexia. The address is as follows:

The Orton Dyslexia Society
724 York Road
Baltimore, MD 21204
Tel: 301-296-0232

JOURNAL OF LEARNING DISABILITIES, P.O. Box 3217, Secaucus, NJ 07096. Tel:800-533-5426; Fax:201-319-9659. This journal, published monthly, features original articles submitted by professionals from various disciplines, editorials, special reports, news, book reviews, abstracts, federal news, letters to the editor, conference calendars, products and meeting reports.

REFERENCES

Abramowitz AJ, Dulcan MK et al. ADHD children's responses to stimulant medication and two intensities of a behavioral intervention. Behavior Modification 1992;16:193-203.

Barkley RA. Attention-Deficit Hyperactivity Disorder: A Handbook for Diagnosis and Treatment. New York, Guildford Press, 1990.

Churchill WS. My Early Life. A Roving Commission. New York, Charles Scribner's Sons, 1930.

Dulcan MK. Treatment of children and adolescents. In: RE Hales, SC Yodofsky, JA Talbott (Eds), The American Psychiatric Press Textbook of Psychiatry, 2nd ed, Washington, DC, American Psychiatric Press, 1994, pp 1209-1250.

Millichap MG. The Effects of the Developmentally Disabled Child on the Family. Roosevelt University, Masters Degree Thesis, Chicago, 1984.

Millichap JG. The Hyperactive Child with Minimal Brain Dysfunction. Questions and Answers. Chicago, Year Book Medical Publishers, 1975.

Millichap NM. Dyslexia: Theories of Causation and Methods of Management, An Historical Perspective. Loyola University of Chicago, Masters Degree Thesis, 1986.

Millichap Nancy M, and Millichap JG. Dyslexia: As the Educator and Neurologist Read It. Springfield, IL, Charles C Thomas, 1986.

Rosenberger PB. Attention deficit. Pediatr Neurol 1991;7:397-405.

CHAPTER 9

MEDICATIONS
FOR ADHD

Medications, and especially central nervous system stimulants, are an important part of treatment of ADHD. The use of stimulants for the treatment of hyperactive behavior in children was first described in 1937, beginning with the amphetamines. Controlled trials of methylphenidate (Ritalin®) in the 1960s demonstrated significant benefits without serious side effects. In addition to a lessening of motor activity, focus and attention were prolonged, and school work, grades and social behavior were improved. In small to moderate doses, methylphenidate benefits learning without impairing creative or flexible thinking. The value of stimulant medication in the management of ADHD has withstood the test of time.

Despite the proven benefits, parents are frequently

skeptical about the use of a drug that facilitates learning and modifies behavior. It is hoped that the following answers to the most common questions will provide a better understanding of the actions and side effects of medications for ADHD and will allay some of the parental fears concerning the use of drugs.

Q: What stimulant medications are available for treatment of ADHD?

A: A list of central nervous stimulant medications available for treatment of ADHD is shown in Table 9-1.

TABLE 9-1. STIMULANT MEDICATIONS USED IN ADHD.

Generic name	Brand name	Tablets (mg)
Methylphenidate	Ritalin	5, 10, 20
	Ritalin-SR	20
d-Amphetamine	Dexedrine	5
	Dexedrine-Sp	5, 10, 15
d & l-Amphetamines	Adderal	5, 10, 20, 30
Pemoline	Cylert	18.75, 37.5, 75

SR, sustained-release; SP, spansule; d & l, dextro & levo.

Ritalin® or its generic form, methylphenidate, is the most widely prescribed central nervous stimulant for the treatment of ADHD. The earliest reported use of stimulant medications for hyperactive children is usually credited to Bradley (1937), who employed first Benzedrine (dl-amphetamine) and later, in 1950, Dexedrine (d-amphetamine). Benzedrine is no longer available, but Dexedrine is prescribed in about 12% of patients. Recently, a mixture of amphetamines has been marketed under the trade name Adderal®, which appears to have properties superior to Dexedrine alone.

Cylert has a different chemical structure from the amphetamines and Ritalin, and it has a longer duration of action. Because of occasional reports of liver toxicity, Cylert is now prescribed as a second line medication for ADHD.

Some differences in potency of the brand or trade preparation, Ritalin,® and the generic form, methylphenidate, have been observed in practice and in clinical trials. The substitution of the generic for the Ritalin brand may result in a change in effectiveness. A reported lack of response to treatment with the generic methylphenidate should prompt a trial of brand-named Ritalin before accepting failure of stimulant therapy. In subsequent references to trials of stimulant medications, the brand or the generic name will be listed depending on which form was prescribed.

Q: How does a stimulant medication have a calming effect?

A: The primary function of a psychostimulant medication is to increase focus and alertness. Structurally, the amphetamines resemble neuro-transmitters, brain chemicals called catecholamines that facilitate the passage of impulses from one nerve cell to another. The exact mode of action of the amphetamine medications is not known. They are thought to increase catecholamine activity in the brain, leading to a build up of the neurotransmitter chemicals, norepinephrine and dopamine, at the synapse junctions between neurons. Methylphenidate is structurally similar to the amphetamines but may have slightly different chemical effects.

The brain has both excitatory and inhibitory motor pathways that are influenced by the neurochemical transmitters. A deficiency in neurotransmitters could weaken inhibition and permit excessive motor activity. In theory, children with ADHD are lacking in brain dopamine and norepinephrine. The so-called "paradoxical" calming effect of psychostimulants may be related to an increase and correction in the levels of these neurotransmitter chemicals in the brain, restoring the function of inhibitory pathways. These chemical effects are thought to normalize motor activity while still preserving and heightening the degree of alertness.

The metabolic pathways in the formation of chatecholamines and the effects of amphetamines are as follows:

TYROSINE --->DOPA--->DOPAMINE--->NOREPINEPHRINE

Enzymes and cofactors, including pyridoxal phosphate and ascorbate, are involved in these pathways. Catecholamines are concentrated in storage vesicles within nerve terminals. Amphetamines displace catecholamines from the storage vesicles, resulting in leakage of neurotransitters from the nerve terminals.

An alternative or supplement to the neurochemical explanation is based on the neuroanatomical location of the action of psychostimulants and their effect on the frontal lobe of the brain, an area known to have an inhibitory influence on motor activity.

Q: What specific benefits may be expected

from treatment with stimulant medications?

A: In addition to a more focused behavior, the child is less distractible, has a longer attention span and is less active and impulsive. Visual perception, eye-hand coordination, drawing and handwriting are improved, school work is more organized, and achievement of better grades is facilitated. The main purpose of the medication is to help learning and cognitive function, not to control behavior.

In one of the earliest controlled studies of the effectiveness of Ritalin®, conducted at Children's Memorial Hospital, NWU, Chicago, 68% of 30 children with ADHD were benefited during a 3-week trial period. Neuropsychological tests showed improvements in intelligence, visual memory, and eye-hand coordination (Millichap JG et al, 1968). A later review of the literature, and reports of a total of 337 children in seven different trials of Ritalin, showed an average of 83% improved (Millichap JG, 1973).

Subsequent reports of trials of methylphenidate (MPH) and other central nervous stimulants, involving close to 5000 children, have continued to demonstrate a positive response in 70 - 80%. Hyperactive behavior, self-esteem, learning, and social and family functioning are improved. Effects of MPH on comorbid oppositional and conduct disorders are variable, some investigators reporting a lack of response (Spencer T et al, 1996), while others note improvement in teacher conduct ratings (DuPaul GJ, Rapport MD, 1993). In general, MPH has a higher frequency of positive effects on ADHD than on comorbid oppositional and conduct disorders. Children who do not respond to medication require a greater emphasis on behavior modification and parent-family counselling (Abramowitz AJ, Dulcan MK et al, 1992).

Q: Can we predict which ADHD patients are most likely to respond to stimulant medication?

A: Children who are most active, impulsive and distractible are most likely to be benefited by methylphenidate (MPH). These predictors of response to MPH were reported in 1973 (Millichap JG) and confirmed in subsequent studies in 1991 (Barkley RA et al) and in 1994 (Handen BL et al, 1994). Although MPH may be indicated in a child with ADD without hyperactivity and impulsivity, a response is more likely when the inattentive child is also hyperactive.

The clinical judgement of the severity of ADHD and improvement observed after a single dose of MPH are useful predictors of a beneficial long-term response.

Factors predictive of response to MPH were examined in 46 children with ADHD treated at the University of Utrecht, The Netherlands (Buitelaar JK et al, 1995). MPH normalized behavior at school in one half the children and behavior at home in one third. Predictors of response to MPH included a high intelligence quotient, severe inattention, and absence of anxiety. Positive behavioral changes, measured by the Abbreviated Conners Rating Scales, after a single 10 mg dose of MPH were predictive of continued improvements after 4 weeks of treatment.

Q: Does methylphenidate affect a child's creativity and flexibility of thinking?

A: Some parents may be concerned that a medication given to help focusing ability and control impulsivity may at the same time reduce creativity and flexibility of a child's thinking. Researchers investigating effects on creativity, measured by the Torrance nonverbal thinking test, found that methylphenidate (MPH) had no adverse effects on creative thinking in 19 boys with ADHD (Funk JB et al, 1993). Control of impulsivity is independent of creativity. Furthermore, flexibility of thinking and speed and accuracy of processing information were improved in studies using acute, single MPH doses of 0.3 and 0.6 mg (Douglas VI et al, 1995). In small to moderate doses, MPH does not impair a child's creativity and flexibility of thinking.

Q: How important is the dose of methylphenidate (MPH) in the response of ADHD? What is the optimal dose range of MPH?

A: The response to methylphenidate (MPH) is related to the dose, especially for tasks requiring attention. Cognitive performance and learning ability are improved by lower doses (0.3 mg/kg) whereas higher doses (1.0 mg/kg) may impair learning but improve social behavior, according to one report (Sprague and Sleator, 1977).

A subsequent study found slightly different effects. The beneficial effects of MPH on academic performance did not vary with dosage, but behavioral improvements were more prolonged with the larger dose (Tannock R et al, 1989).

The lower dose (0.3 mg/kg) taken in the morning produced

both academic and behavioral improvements that were no longer present in the afternoon. A higher morning dose (1.0 mg/kg) was followed by improvements in behavior that were sustained, and academic improvements that disappeared, by the afternoon. Side effects involving an increase in pulse rate and blood pressure were observed only with the larger dose.

More recent studies investigated the effects of MPH at four different dose levels, 5, 10, 15, and 20 mg. (Rapport MD et al, 1994). The effects on classroom functioning, including on-task attention, assignment completion, and teacher ratings, were related to the dose of MPH. Accuracy of work was increased at all dose levels, and task completion was significantly greater at single doses above 5 mg. In children failing to respond to low dose MPH, focus of attention was responsive to dose increments whereas behavior and academic achievement were not improved by larger doses.

These well controlled research studies indicate that smaller doses of MPH will benefit both academic performance and behavior and are generally preferable to a single larger dose, but the action is short lived and the dose must be repeated to sustain effectiveness. In attempting to determine an optimal dose for each individual child, the duration of action on academic, cognitive, and behavioral performance must be evaluated.

At the Scottish Rite Children's Medical Center, Atlanta, GA, the effects on attention and learning of 2 different doses (0.3 and 0.8 mg/kg) of methylphenidate (MPH) were evaluated in 23 children, aged 7 to 11 years, with ADHD. An attention continuous performance task was improved with the low dose MPH, and impulsivity measured by the number of commission errors was reduced. On nonverbal learning and memory tasks, the easy level of task performance was improved equally with either dose of MPH, whereas the hard task was performed better only with the high dose (O'Toole K, Dulcan M et al, 1997).

Attention and impulsivity are benefited by low doses of MPH, but higher doses may be required to improve retention and recall of complex nonverbal information. Cognitive function as well as behavior are sensitive to stimulant medication, but doses must be individualized and titrated for each patient.

MPH is generally administered two or three times a day, after breakfast, at lunch-time at school, and if necessary, at 3 to 4 o'clock in the afternoon. The initial dose is usually 5 mg, 2 or 3 times daily, independent of the age or weight of the child, at 5 years of age and older. Dose-response does not vary with body weight (Rapport MD, Denney C, 1997).

If an increase in dose is considered necessary, increments should be small, 2.5 mg daily, at intervals not shorter than one week. In my experience, doses larger than 10 mg, 2 or 3 times daily, are generally unhelpful and are often accompanied by unwanted side effects. Rarely, a child may require 15 or 20 mg in the morning for optimal effects on learning. Generally, if small or moderate doses of MPH are ineffective, the diagnosis and choice of treatment should be reassessed, and some alternative form of stimulant or change in medication should be considered.

Q: Twice daily versus three times daily MPH dose schedule. Which is better?

A: Methylphenidate administered twice daily benefits behavior and learning of ADHD children in the classroom but not in the home. Three times daily schedule of doses may facilitate completion of homework assignments and benefit parent-child relations. In lower school grades the twice daily dose schedule may be adequate, but in higher grades with a heavier academic load, an additional MPH dose at 3 or 4 o'clock may be required, provided sleeping habits are not disturbed. Furthermore, the third dose may prevent any MPH rebound effect experienced on returning home from school.

At the University of Chicago, the efficacy and side effects of twice daily (bid) and three times daily (tid) MPH dosing schedules (mean dose, 8 mg [0.3 mg/kg]) in 25 boys with ADHD were compared in a 5-week, placebo-controlled, crossover evaluation. Three times daily dosing provided greater improvement than the bid schedule on Conners Parent and Teacher Rating scales, and the incidence of side effects, including insomnia, was not increased (Stein MA et al, 1996).

At the Hospital for Sick Children, Toronto, Canada, a placebo-controlled study of 91 children receiving MPH, titrated to 0.7 mg/kg twice daily over a period of 4 months, found that symptoms of ADHD and comorbid oppositional disorder improved while at school but not on returning home. Rebound side effects observed by parents included sadness, behavioral deterioration, irritability, withdrawal lethargy, violent behavior, and mild mania (Schachar RJ et al, 1997).

Children in the Toronto study, receiving relatively large doses of MPH twice daily, experienced frequent rebound symptoms on return home in the afternoon, whereas a three times daily schedule and lower doses of MPH in the Chicago study were associated with sustained improvement in behavior rating scales and much fewer side effects. Furthermore, an evening free from parent-child conflict and a homework assignment satisfactorily completed, as a result of a third dose of MPH, can lead to improved self-esteem and better classroom performance.

Q: Is MPH safe and effective in preschool children with ADHD?

A: The majority of the studies of methylphenidate in ADHD have been conducted in children of 5 years and older. Parents of preschool ADHD children are often advised to rely on behavior modification counselling, a method of management which is rarely effective. Physicians have been reluctant to prescribe stimulants for younger children because of the paucity of scientifically controlled studies. The following report should help to dispell concerns and encourage a wider but still carefully monitored usage of MPH in preschoolers.

At the University of Ottawa, Canada, 31 children, aged 4 to 6 years, with ADHD and comorbid oppositional disorder, were treated with MPH (0.3 and 0.5 mg/kg twice daily) in a double-blind, placebo-controlled investigation. During treatment with MPH, significant improvements were obtained on a cognitive measure (number of correct responses on the Gordon Vigilance Task), on parent ratings of child's behavior, and tasks measuring the ability to complete a paper-and-pencil assignment. Improved performance during MPH treatment was also noted on measures of impulsivity-hyperactivity and conduct. Side effects, stomachache, headache, anxiety and sadness, increased in frequency and severity with the higher dose of MPH (Musten LM et al, 1997).

Q: Is MPH effective in ADHD adolescents?

A: The symptoms of ADHD in adolescents are almost identical to those during childhood, and the effectiveness and side effects of methylphenidate (MPH) are also similar in the two age groups. The dose of MPH should not automatically be increased in accordance with age and weight gains. ADHD patients who develop worsening of symptoms in high school should receive psychosocial counselling and/or tutoring before advising an increase in dose of stimulant.

At the Western Psychiatric Institute, University of Pittsburgh, PA, the effectiveness of MPH, 0.3 mg/kg, in ADHD was compared during childhood and adolescence in a retrospective follow-up study of 16 patients enrolled in summer treatment programs. Of 12 objective measures of academic performance and social behavior and counselor and teacher ratings, only 3 showed significant changes in MPH responsiveness from childhood to adolescence (Smith BH et al, 1998).

Stimulant medication is equally effective in ADHD during childhood and adolescence, provided that environment and activities remain constant. Patterns of psychosocial adversity and comorbidity with conduct, mood, and anxiety disorders are almost identical.

If substance abuse becomes a problem in adolescence, it is independent of ADHD (Biederman J et al, 1998). Treatment with buproprion, which has a lower abuse potential, is substituted for stimulant medication in some centers (Riggs PD, 1998). Tricyclic antidepressants are considered too dangerous for use in impulsive youths, with risk of illicit drug interaction and high incidence of death with overdose.

Q: What is the child's perspective of stimulant medication for ADHD and its effect on peer relations?

A: In a study of 45 children receiving stimulant medication for ADHD, researchers at the Boston Children's Hospital found that 89% felt that the medication was helpful. Improved concentration and ability to sit still in the classroom were the most frequently reported benefits. Decreased appetite and difficulty falling asleep were the most common side effects. Only 5 (11%) children would prefer to stop taking medication, mainly because of the inconvenience of the lunchtime dose at school. Those taking a sustained release or long acting stimulant found the treatment acceptable (Bowen J et al, 1991).

ADHD children frequently have problems in social relationships with their peers. They are more aggressive, domineering, intrusive and talkative, but they lack ability to communicate with others socially. Their inner or internal "locus of control" of behavior is defective, and they have a more external locus of behavior control than normal children. They view a failure to relate to others as outside their personal control and due to external factors. ADHD children, especially those with aggressive tendencies, are often rejected by their peers (Barkley RA, 1990; Millichap MG, 1998).

The effects of methylphenidate (MPH) on social behavior and peer interactions have been investigated in several studies, notably those of Carol Whalen, Barbara Henker and colleagues at the University of California, Irvine and Los Angeles. During unstructured activities in an outside summer program, 15 of 24 hyperactive children, ages 6 to 11 years, treated with MPH (0.3 and 0.6 mg/kg), showed medication-related reduction in negative behaviors. Younger children were benefited more than older children, and the effects were dose related, using low and moderate amounts. MPH in conservative doses benefits behavior and social interaction with peers without causing social withdrawal (Whalen CK et al, 1987).

Treatment with stimulant medications increases compliance with parental and teacher requests and improves peer acceptance and social interaction. The reduction in aggressive behavior associated with a positive medication effect is an important factor in the improved sociability with peers (Whalen CK et al, 1989; Barkley RA, 1990).

Q: What is the duration of action of the various stimulant drugs, and are the sustained-release preparations effective?

A: The time of onset and duration of action of stimulant medications vary with the drug, its form, and the dose. Table 9-2 shows an approximation of these times for each preparation.

Ritalin® (methylphenidate) has a rapid onset of action and relatively short duration of effect. Tablets have to be administered every 3.5 to 4 hours during the daytime to maintain an effect. Any side effect is also short-lived, an advantage that offsets the inconvenience of multiple doses. Ritalin can be given when needed as an aid to education, and treatment may be skipped at weekends and on vacations.

Ritalin SR 20® (methylphenidate sustained release) is designed to be long acting, approximately 6 - 8 hours, but absorption is variable and sometimes erratic, depending on the individual. Rapid and high blood concentrations may result if the tablet is chewed rather than swallowed. Studies have found the sustained release preparation to have a delayed onset of action and to be less effective than the standard tablet, especially in the first one or two hours after ingestion. It may be tried in a child who experiences behavioral rebound with the regular tablet, or in situations where in-school administration of medication is impractical or undesirable. Adults sometimes prefer Ritalin SR because it may have less tendency to induce anxiety and restlessness, side effects not often seen in children.

TABLE 9-2. DURATION OF ACTION OF STIMULANT MEDICATIONS FOR ADHD

Drug Preparation	Time of Onset hrs.	Duration hrs.
Ritalin tablet	0.25	3.5 - 4
Ritalin SR 20	0.5	6 - 8
Dexedrine tablet	0.3 - 0.5	4
Dexedrine spansule	0.5	6 - 8
Adderal tablet	0.3 - 0.5	3.5 - 6
Cylert tablet	2	8 - 12

Dexedrine® (dextroamphtamine), a short acting tablet or elixir, may have a slightly longer duration of action and a slightly delayed onset compared to Ritalin.

Dexedrine Spansule® (dextroamphetamine) has a longer duration of action than the tablet form. It usually lasts for 6 - 8 hours, but its action varies with the individual, sometimes extending through the evening.

Adderal® (d- & d,l-amphetamines), a mixture of amphetamines, was first marketed for the treatment of ADHD in 1994. Experience with this drug is relatively short, but one recent controlled study demonstrated a slightly longer duration of action than MPH or Ritalin (Swanson JM et al, 1998). It may have a smoother, more sustained effect in some individuals and less tendency to withdrawal side-effects.

Cylert® (pemoline), a long-acting tablet, taken orally every morning. The once a day dosage avoids the inconvenience of taking a drug at school. The effect is slow in onset but long in duration, lasting up to 12 hours. An increasing number of reports of acute liver failure are cause for concern. Cylert is a second line treatment choice, and liver function must be monitored regularly. Despite this inconvenience, some patients and particularly high school students prefer Cylert to the shorter acting stimulants.

Q: For how long should stimulant medication be continued, and is it overused?

A: Parents are frequently concerned that treatment with stimulants has to be continued indefinitely. In practice, the average child will receive treatment intermittently for 3 years. Some will be able to discontinue medication after one year and others may need therapy for 5 years or longer.

Duration of stimulant therapy is determined by trial and error. Drug holidays during extended summer vacations permit reappraisal of the need for medication on return to school. Teacher reports regarding attention and behavior should be obtained within one to two weeks after starting a new term. In children whose symptoms of ADHD are persistent, the physician should be consulted about renewal of a prescription.

Researchers find little evidence of abuse or overuse of stimulant medication in the treatment of ADHD during childhood and adolescence (Goldman LS et al, 1998). Based on DEA production quotas for methylphenidate (MPH), a 2.8-fold increase in usage between 1990 and 1995 is far less than the media claims of a 6-fold increased usage. Approximately 2.8% (1.5 million) US children aged 5 to 18 received MPH for ADHD in 1995. The increased usage was related to more prolonged treatment, more girls treated, and adolescents receiving medication for ADD (Safer DJ et al, 1996).

Q: What are the effects of long-term usage of stimulants on ADHD outcome?

A: Studies of long-term, uninterrupted stimulant therapy are infrequent. One recent report of a 15 month controlled trial of amphetamine in 62 children, aged 6 to 11 years, with ADHD showed continued improvements in behavior and learning ability, with no serious side effects.

A multicenter placebo-controlled trial of amphetamine treatment for ADHD in Sweden found significant improvements in attention, hyperactivity, and disruptive behaviors, and a mean change in IQ of +4.5 after more than 9 months of amphetamine sulfate. Side effects included decreased appetite in 56%, abdominal pain in 32%, tics in 29%, and visual hallucinations requiring dose reduction or withdrawal in 5%. Abdominal pain and tics occurred with equal frequency in the placebo group, and only one of 4 children with tics at base-line had an increase in symptoms during amphetamine (15 mg/day) treatment (Gillberg C et al, 1997).

The children in the Swedish study had a high incidence of comorbid diagnoses (42%), including pervasive developmental disorders, mild retardation, and oppositional defiant disorder. Longterm trials of stimulants in ADHD with less comorbidity would be expected to show greater beneficial effects and less side effects. The unusually high incidence of tic disorders in both treated and untreated children was remarkable.

A collaborative multimodal treatment study of children with ADHD, the MTA, described by NIMH collaborators (Jensen PS et al, 1997), will examine long-term effectiveness of medication vs behavioral treatment vs both in 576 children treated for 14 months and reassessed for 24 months. The first patients were enrolled in 1994 and the last will complete the trial in 1998. The results of this multicenter study will provide further data on the longterm effects and safety of stimulant therapy.

Q: Could continued usage of MPH through adolescence and young adulthood reduce the risks of motor vehicle accidents related to

ADHD?

A: ADHD young adults are twice as likely to be cited for unlawful speeding, have more crashes, and more accidents involving bodily injury, when compared to non-ADHD adult control subjects. They are more likely to have licenses suspended, and their driving habits and performance are poorer despite adequate driving knowledge. These statistics were obtained from a study of motor vehicle skills, risks, and accidents in 25 young adults with ADHD compared to controls, aged 17 to 30 years, followed at the University of Massachusetts Medical Center, Worcester, MA (Barkley RA et al, 1996).

This study confirms previous reports of an increased incidence of motor vehicle accidents and injury among ADHD young adults. The findings support a proposed need for continued treatment and supervision of adolescents with ADHD into adulthood, particularly in those with persistent problems in motor control and impulsive behavior.

SIDE EFFECTS OF STIMULANT MEDICATIONS

Q: What are the side effects of methylphenidate (Ritalin®) and how prevalent are they?

A: Side effects occur with all medications. Drugs without side effects are probably ineffective. We distinguish between mild and transient side effects and severe and chronic toxic reactions. Side effects that occur with methylphenidate (MPH) are generally mild and transient. Prolonged usage of MPH has failed to uncover any life threatening toxic reactions.

The list and frequency of occurrence of the most common side effects of MPH are shown in Table 9-3. They are usually dose-related. These data are based on personal experience as well as reviews of the medical literature, including studies by Barkley et al (1991) and Ahmann PA et al (1993), using Parent and Teacher Questionnaires. Many of the reported side effects occur without drugs or during placebo trials. The significance of reported MPH-related side effects must be assessed by comparison with symptoms occurring during drug "holidays," at weekends and on vacations.

TABLE 9-3. SIDE EFFECTS OF METHYLPHENIDATE

Side Effect	Dose Related Occurrence (%)	
	Low dose	Moderate dose
Decreased appetite	40%	60%
Increased appetite	5	5
Insomnia	10	15
Stomachaches	10	15
Weight loss	5	10
Headaches	3	5
Tics	3	5
Mood change	2	7
Growth delay	1	5

Decreased appetite occurs in about 50% of patients taking MPH. The child eats lunch sparingly but often has a good appetite for dinner. If weight loss occurs, it usually stabilizes after 4 weeks, provided the dosage of

MPH is small to moderate. Dietary supplements offered at breakfast and bedtime are usually sufficient to compensate for the reduced appetite at lunchtime. Appetite stimulation may occur in a small percentage of patients; ironically, this occurs usually in those who are overweight before starting treatment.

Sleep disturbance (insomnia) occurs mainly when MPH is taken after 4 o'clock in the afternoon or when higher doses are used. A modification of the timing or size of dose permits a return to normal sleep habits.

Stomachaches and headaches are sometimes troublesome, necessitating either reduction in dosage or a change in diet. Headaches due to tension and school frustrations are often relieved when MPH is begun.

Tics, mood changes, and growth delay are side effects that may cause greater concern, and these are discussed in more detail.

Q: Is MPH-induced growth delay a real problem or a media exaggerated concern?

A: A suppressant effect of stimulant drugs on the growth of hyperactive children was reported in 1972 (Safer D et al). The annual growth lag was minimal (1.0-1.5 cm) and occurred only when larger doses (>20 mg daily) of methylphenidate (MPH) or dextro-amphetamine were given regularly for two or more years. An analysis of heights of 50 children in my own practice failed to confirm a growth suppressant effect of MPH, when more conservative doses were used and treatment was interrupted at weekends and on vacations (Millichap JG, 1977).

Growth delays caused by MPH are a major concern

of parents because of excess media attention to this side effect. In reality, growth is delayed only with higher doses and when weight loss is significant. A rebound in growth to normal levels may be expected when treatment is interrupted, and a permanent growth suppression does not occur. Indeed, a stimulation of growth has been observed in some younger patients in my own practice.

Q: What are the mood changes sometimes associated with MPH and how can they be avoided?

A: Irritability, a tendency to cry easily, impassive expression and dysphoria or sadness are some of the mood changes reported in children taking methylphenidate (MPH) and other stimulant medications. "My child looks like a zombi," is a parent's usual response to this side effect. Depressive reactions to MPH occur mainly with larger doses (20 mg, 2 or 3x daily, or higher) and in children with a family history of depression. Irritability may also occur as a "rebound" phenomenon, on return home from school in the afternoon. A small dose of MPH (5 mg) given at 3 PM or a reduction in the lunchtime dose will usually correct this withdrawal effect.

The dose-related dysphoric (depressive) effect of MPH and other stimulants is usually accompanied by a loss of appetite and weight. It can be avoided by either reduction in dosage or a change to an alternative medication.

Q: What is the treatment for tics developing

during stimulant therapy for ADHD?

A: Tics or Tourette syndrome may develop as a side effect of stimulant therapy for ADHD, especially in children with a prior history or family predisposition to tic disorders. Rarely, obsessive compulsive disorder is also associated with tics and MPH therapy. The frequency of occurrence of transient tics is approximately 5%, or 1 in 20 patients treated. Some have estimated that fewer than 1% of ADHD children treated with methylphenidate will develop a tic disorder, whereas the risk is closer to 10% in patients with a pre-existing tendency to tics (Denckla MB et al, 1976).

Parents should be alert to the symptoms of tics or Tourette syndrome, and the physician should be notified if tics develop. Stimulants of all types, including caffeine-containing beverages and chocolate, should generally be avoided in patients with a tendency to tics. Withdrawal of the stimulant is usually followed by remission but rarely, tics may persist and require therapy. MPH appears less likely to induce persistent tic exacerbations than amphetamines.

At the National Institute of Mental Health, Bethesda, MD, the effects of methylphenidate (MPH) and dextroamphetamine (DEX) on tic severity in 20 boys with ADHD and comorbid Tourette syndrome were investigated in a 9-week, placebo-controlled, double-blind crossover study. Tic severity was significantly greater during treatment with high doses of both MPH (20-25 mg twice daily) and DEX (12.5-22.5 mg twice daily). ADHD symptoms were benefited by both stimulants, and treatment was continued for 1 to 3 years in 14 of the 20 patients. Tic exacerbations were reversible, and MPH was better tolerated than DEX (Castellanos FX et al, 1997). Conventional doses of MPH (0.1-0.3 mg/kg) produced dramatic improvement in behavior in children with ADHD and tic disorders, in a study at *State University of New York, Stony Brook, NY* (Nolan EE, Gadow KD, 1997).

The occurrence of tics with MPH, amphetamines or pemoline is generally dose-related, occurring mainly with larger doses. The lowest effective dose of stimulant should be used, and increases in dosage should be made slowly. If a reduction in dose is not quickly followed by a remission of tics, then the stimulant should be discontinued.

Clonidine (Catapres®) is an alternative medication prescribed in children with ADHD complicated by tics. Combinations of clonidine and stimulant drugs are usually not advised, since serious cardiac-related adverse effects have been reported. MPH should be withdrawn before clonidine is introduced (see Chap 6 and a subsequent section on use of clonidine for tics).

Q: What is the "behavioral rebound" associated with MPH treatment for ADHD?

A: Some children with ADHD treated with morning and noon doses of methylphenidate (MPH) will function satisfactorily at school, but their behavior relapses when they return home in the afternoon. This deterioration in behavior, sometimes exceeding the pre-treatment condition, is called "behavioral rebound." It is characterized by an increase in hyperactivity and impulsiveness and in addition, the child becomes irritable, tends to cry easily, and may have temper outbursts. In a sample of 21 children treated with two doses of MPH, about one third were affected by behavioral deterioration in late afternoon or evening, and the degree of rebound was variable from day to day (Johnston C et al, 1985).

Treatment options for behavioral rebound include the addition of a small dose (2.5 or 5 mg) of MPH at 3 or 4 o'clock in the afternoon, or a reduction in the noontime dosage. Alternatively, a change to a longer acting stimulant such as Adderal may be found satisfactory.

Q: Can methylphenidate cause or exacerbate seizures?

A: The relation of seizures to treatment with MPH is controversial. A tendency to seizures demonstrated by an abnormal electroencephalogram occurs in 7% of children with ADHD, and clinical seizures are occasionally reported in children taking larger doses of MPH and other stimulants. Patients taking combinations of MPH and antidepressants, such as imipramine, buproprion, or sertraline, are especially at risk of seizures.

The Physicians' Desk Reference (PDR) includes a contraindication to the use of Ritalin as follows: "There is some clinical evidence that Ritalin may lower the convulsive threshold in patients with prior history of seizures, with prior EEG abnormalities in the absence of seizures, and, very rarely, in absence of history of seizures and no prior EEG evidence of seizures. Safe concomitant use of anticonvulsants and Ritalin has not been established. In the presence of seizures, the drug should be discontinued."

While the PDR cautions against the use of MPH in patients with epilepsy and ADHD, most neurologists will prescribe MPH or other stimulant therapy, provided that seizures are controlled with adequate levels of antiepileptic medications. In studies of children with well controlled epilepsy and ADHD, the addition of MPH to antiepileptic drug therapy had no adverse effect on seizure control or on the EEG. MPH can be a safe and effective treatment for ADHD complicated by epilepsy provided that seizures are controlled by anticonvulsant medication (McBride MC et al, 1986; Feldman H et al, 1989; Gross-Tsur V et al, 1997). MPH should be discontinued or the dosage reduced, if seizures recur (Millichap, JG, Swisher CN, 1997). Combinations of MPH and some antidepressants will increase the risk of seizures and should be avoided.

At Wright State University, School of Medicine, Dayton, OH, a 13-year-old boy with ADHD and depressive reaction had a tonic-clonic seizure 1 week after the antidepressant sertraline (50 mg/day) was added to treatment with MPH (80 mg/day). MPH dosage had been gradually increased without seizure occurrence over a period of a year before the addition of sertraline. The EEG was normal. Sertraline was discontinued, and MPH was continued unchanged with no recurrence of seizures (Feeney DJ, Klykylo WM, 1997).

An EEG is indicated before prescribing MPH or other stimulant therapy for ADHD if a child has a personal or family history of seizures, or if a parent, teacher, psychologist, or physician has remarked on recurrent staring or episodes of confusion. An epileptiform EEG is an indication for a trial of antiepileptic medication (eg. carbamazepine) before starting treatment with MPH. If symptoms of ADHD persist, then the addition of MPH may be justified. In circumstances where antiepileptic drugs are not tolerated and no clinical seizures have occurred, a trial of small doses of MPH may be initiated followed by EEG monitoring at intervals. MPH may be continued in the absence of seizures or worsening of the EEG.

Although MPH may exacerbate epileptiform activity in the EEG of patients susceptible to seizures, studies in non-seizure patients with ADHD have demonstrated a normalizing effect. Using EEG spectral analysis in 23 boys with ADHD, regional improvements in the EEG during MPH treatment were associated with improvements in tasks involving reading, coding, and visual-motor perception. The EEG as a measure of MPH effects in ADHD requires further study (Swartwood MO et al, 1998).

Care must be taken in the choice of antiepileptic medication in children with ADHD. Certain drugs, particularly phenobarbital, will exacerbate hyperactivity, and many of the antiepileptic medications can affect learning and memory at therapeutic dose levels.

Q: What are some of the less well recognized side effects of methylphenidate and other stimulants?

A: The following are side effects of MPH that occur infrequently but which may require reduction in dosage or withdrawal of the drug and substitution of an alternative therapy:

• Increased hyperactivity occurs in 5% of children treated with MPH. Other forms of stimulant medications will have the same effect in these individual patients, and a different class of treatment will be indicated. The antihypertensive agent, clonidine, or antidepressant, buproprion, is an alternative choice of drug therapy.

• Obsessive compulsive disorder (OCD) is a rarely reported side effect of MPH, and generally associated with tics. Dextroamphetamine has been implicated more often than MPH. The incidence of stimulant-induced OCD may be higher than the literature documents.

An 8-year-old boy developed a transient but severely debilitating OCD after 2 weeks of treatment with MPH (10 mg/daily) for a mild, uncomplicated ADHD. He also developed tics involving the head and neck. The past history was negative for psychiatric comorbidity, recent streptococcal infection, and familial anxiety disorders. Withdrawal of MPH was followed by gradual recovery from OCD over a 3 month period (Kouris S, 1998).

• Trichotillomania, a compulsive habit of hair-pulling from the scalp, eyebrows and even eyelashes, is an occasional side effect of MPH. In one study involving 3 boys, symptoms abated slowly or diminished in 2, despite continuation of the MPH. The habit persisted in one after switching to imipramine therapy (Martin A, 1998).

The majority of cases of trichotillomania (TT) are associated with depressive symptoms and not ADHD, and stimulant medications are not the cause. Females are affected 10 times more often than males, and symptoms can persist into adulthood, despite behavioral and medication therapy (Keuthen NJ et al, 1998).

• Finger tip skin and nail biting occurs in 1 to 3% of patients after starting MPH and appears to be related to the treatment. A reduction in dosage may be sufficient to correct this side effect.

• Redness and burning sensation in the ears, face and hands are side effects of MPH in 1% of children. Peeling of the skin of the palms is a rare observation and a suspect but not proven side effect of MPH. A reduction in dose and sometimes, withdrawal of the drug may be necessary.

• Generalized skin rash is a rare side effect, occurring in less than 0.5% of children. I have never seen a serious skin rash with MPH, but with any drug-related skin rash, treatment should be discontinued.

• Complete blood counts and liver function tests are generally recommended as a routine, at 6 month intervals or if indicated by specific symptoms, if MPH is continued without intermission during school and vacation times. I have not encountered a case of blood or liver toxicity secondary to MPH or Ritalin, and routine testing is not generally necessary if medication is withheld at weekends and on vacations.

• Heart palpitations, rapid pulse, chest pain, and elevated blood pressure may occur, particularly with larger doses of MPH. An electrocardiogram and cardiology consultation should be ordered, and the stimulant medication should be discontinued or the dose reduced.

• A possible effect on the immune system by MPH in larger doses (30-45 mg/day) is reported in an isolated study (Auci DL et al, 1997). MPH induced a twofold increase in IgE levels in 3 of 6 boys treated, as well as other signs of immune system hypersensitivity. Larger doses of MPH should be avoided when possible, and especially in patients with IgE-mediated asthma, allergic rhinitis, and other atopic diseases. Drugs used in asthma have been implicated as a cause of ADHD. If significant, this study warns of a possible adverse effect of MPH on the outcome of asthma and other allergic diseases.

Q: What are the advantages and risks of Cylert® in treatment of ADHD?

A: Cylert (pemoline) is a longer acting stimulant medication than Ritalin, Dexedrine or Adderal, and a single daily morning dose is sufficient to maintain a response in children with ADHD. The inconvenience of taking medication at school is avoided. The benefits and side effects are similar to those reported with shorter acting stimulants, except for the need to monitor liver function closely. Occasional reports of serious liver toxicity have interrupted the popularity of Cylert, and the drug is no longer prescribed as a first line therapy for ADHD.

In the first trials of Cylert in the early 1970s, elevations of liver enzymes were noted in about 2% of patients treated and tested routinely. Interruption of treatment was followed by return of liver function to normal. With more prolonged usage and experience, some patients were found to have more persistent liver enzyme elevations. By the early 1990s, occasional cases of severe liver damage associated with Cylert were reported to the Food and Drug Administration (FDA), and in late 1995, Cylert was no longer recommended as a first line therapy for ADHD.

The medical literature reports of Cylert-associated cases of liver damage have been reviewed and some were linked to other related causes. Of 4 cases reviewed in early 1997, one was a deliberate Cylert overdose, and one had pre-existing liver disease. Of these cases, only two appeared justified and associated directly with Cylert (Shevell M, Schreiber R, 1997). The possibility of a drug-induced autoimmune mechanism and hepatitis was suggested in recent reports of another 5 cases of severe liver failure associated with Cylert (Rosh JR et al, 1998; Hochman JA et al, 1998).

Patients treated with Cylert are required to have regular blood tests for liver function at monthly intervals. Symptoms of nausea, appetite loss, vomiting and jaundice are indications of liver dysfunction, requiring immediate withdrawal of Cylert. The drug should not be administered in patients with a previous history of liver dysfunction or with a personal or family history of autoimmune disease (rheumatoid arthritis, diabetes, lupus, multiple sclerosis). Prolonged uninterrupted usage is probably inadvisable.

Despite the warnings issued with prescriptions for Cylert, some patients have elected to continue treatment, the benefits apparently outweighing the risks. In addition to regular liver function monitoring, patients are urged to take drug holidays when possible and not to combine other medications with Cylert.

ALTERNATIVE MEDICATIONS TO STIMULANTS

Approximately 20 to 25% of children with ADHD fail to respond to stimulant medication or have side effects or conditions contraindicating their use. Table 9-4 lists the generic and brand names of alternative drugs and the strength of tablets or other forms.

Alternative medications for ADHD that may be substituted when stimulant therapy fails include the antihypertensive agents, clonopin (Catapres) or guanfacine (Tenex), the antidepressants, buproprion (Wellbutrin), imipramine (Tofranil), and desipramine (Norpramin), and the anticonvulsant, carbamazepine

(Tegretol, Carbatrol). Buspirone (BuSpar), an antianxiety agent, has also been used successfully in limited trials (Malhotra S, Santosh PJ, 1998).

TABLE 9-4. ALTERNATIVE MEDICATIONS TO STIMULANTS IN TREATMENT OF ADHD

Generic Name	Brand Name	Strength (mg)	
Clonidine	Catapres	tablet	0.1
	Catapres TTS-1	patch	0.1
Guanfacine	Tenex	tablet	1.0
Buproprion	Wellbutrin	tablet	75, 100
	Wellbutrin SR	tablet	100, 150
Imipramine	Tofranil	tablet	10, 25
Desipramine	Norpramin	tablet	10, 25
Carbamazepine	Tegretol	tablet	100, 200
		susp'n	100/5 ml
	Tegretol-XR	tablet	100, 200
	Carbatrol-XR	caps	200, 300

Each of these drugs has specific indications in addition to ADHD. These include the occurrence of comorbid disorders such as tics, oppositional defiance and conduct disorders, and seizures. The choice of medication is dependent not only on efficacy but also on the type and prevalence of reported side effects. In treating children with ADHD, the safety of a medication and absence of serious adverse reactions are of foremost importance in the physician's selection.

Q: What are the indications for using

clonidine   or   guanfacine?

A: *Clonidine* (Catapres®) is a second line treatment for ADHD and is indicated primarily in patients with a history or complication of tics or Tourette syndrome. Behavioral symptoms of ADHD and tics are expected to respond, but inattentiveness and distractibility may persist. Children with comorbid oppositional defiance disorder, anger and low frustration tolerance may be benefited. Drowsiness and fatigue are the most frequent side effects, but given at bedtime to a child with poor sleeping habits, a clonidine side effect may convert to a benefit.

The initial daily dose is small, beginning with one quarter or one half tablet (0.025 - 0.05 mg) one hour after the evening meal or one hour before bedtime. At least 10 days to 2 weeks should be allowed before expecting optimal effects of clonidine and before the dose is increased. If no benefit is obtained after 2 weeks, the daily dose may be increased by one half tablet in the morning after breakfast, provided the child is not drowsy. A further increase of one quarter or one half tablet in the afternoon, on return home from school, may be made if necessary, but increments should be made slowly and not sooner than 5 to 7 day intervals. The optimal dose tolerated in children, 5 to 14 years of age, is usually 0.1 to 0.15 mg daily, but larger amounts are sometimes required.

When clonidine is first prescribed, parents and teachers are advised to be patient while judging the response. Unlike methylphenidate, that acts within hours, the beneficial effects of clonidine on ADHD may be delayed for days or weeks.

Clonidine treatment should not be interrupted at weekends. Sudden withdrawal of larger doses may cause blood pressure elevation or "rebound," hyperactivity, headache, agitation, or exacerbated tics. If treatment is omitted during long vacations, withdrawal should be made slowly and tapered over 4 to 7 days.

Occasional serious, sometimes fatal, reactions to clonidine have been reported when taken in combination with methylphenidate or other stimulant. Before introducing clonidine, stimulant medication should be discontinued, pending further investigation of these reports.

Four cases of adverse reactions to clonidine, administered in combination with MPH or Dexedrine, in children aged 8 to 10 years, are reported from the University of California, LA (Cantwell DP et al, 1997). One patient taking clonidine 0.1 mg 3x daily and MPH 20 mg 2x daily became sedated and fatigued, the blood pressure and pulse were 30% below baseline readings, an electrocardiogram showed slowing and irregular heart rhythms, and the Holter heart monitor recorded an irregular and slow heart rate in sleep.

A second patient, while on clonidine 0.1 mg PM and Dexedrine 12.5 mg daily, forgot to take one clonidine dose. After rollerblading for 10 minutes she became tremulous, her breathing and swallowing were impaired, she looked terrified, her respiration and pulse were abnormally rapid, she became combative, hallucinated, and was disorientated and febrile. The next morning she had recovered and had no memory for the event.

A third patient, on clonidine 0.15 mg PM, MPH 50 mg/daily, and lithium, had a slow pulse and an abnormal electrocardiogram with signs of heart block. Patient 4 had recurrent episodes of fainting related to exercise during treatment with a clonidine patch, 0.2 mg every 5 days. He complained of faintness, passed out, convulsed, and died of cardiac arrest after swimming for 45 minutes. An autopsy revealed a previously undiagnosed congenital heart malformation with stenosis (narrowing) of the left coronary artery. Clonidine blood levels were normal.

The following guidelines for use of clonidine in the treatment of ADHD are recommended:
• Avoid combined therapy with MPH, other stimulants, or antidepressants.
• Screen for previous history of heart disease, and examine heart sounds, pulse, and blood pressure. Obtain EKG and cardiac consultation for abnormal readings, murmurs, or exercise-related syncopal symptoms.
• Dose changes should not exceed 0.05 mg every 5 to 7 days.
• The safety and effectiveness of clonidine and Catapres-TTS® in children has not been endorsed by the FDA, and the TTS-patch (Transdermal Therapeutic System) form of administration is best avoided until more clinical trials are completed.
• Children who have taken clonidine more than a few weeks should not stop the drug abruptly. Withdrawal symptoms, including increased blood pressure, anxiety and agitation, may result.

Guanfacine (Tenex®) is an antihypertensive agent with action and side effects similar to clonidine. Guanfacine may have slightly less sedative effect than clonidine and a longer duration of action.

Imipramine (Tofranil®) and **Desipramine** (Norpramin®) are tricyclic antidepressants (TCAs) sometimes prescribed as a second-line treatment of

ADHD. TCAs have been recommended for those patients who do not respond to stimulants or who develop significant depression on stimulants, or for the treatment of ADHD symptoms in patients with tics, Tourette syndrome, or comorbid depression (Dulcan MK, 1994). Cognitive improvement is not as great as for stimulants. TCAs are also used for nocturnal enuresis, obsessive-compulsive disorder, anxiety, sleep disorders, and depression. Side effects include dry mouth, blurred vision, sedation, and effects on the heart and blood pressure.

Caution is advised in the use of TCAs in the management of ADHD or enuresis in children. Deaths have occurred from accidental or suicidal overdose of TCAs. *Of greater concern is the risk of sudden death recently reported in children taking TCAs, especially desipramine, at usual clinical doses.* Although EKG monitoring seems prudent, it is of doubtful value in predicting risk of fatal reaction to a TCA.

A review of 24 studies, published from various medical centers between 1967 and 1996, and involving 730 children and adolescents treated with TCAs for psychiatric disorders, showed increases in blood pressure and heart rate and changes in the electrocardiogram as a result of usual therapeutic doses. Complaints of light-headedness or headaches signal the need for a check of vital signs, EKG, and TCA blood levels (Wilens TE et al, 1996).

Children engaged in sporting activities should be closely examined for cardiac-related side effects when taking TCAs or, preferably, alternative and safer treatments should be substituted. Although the cardiovascular side effects are generally minor, occasional reports of sudden death are a major concern.

The following two case reports from the Children's Hospital, Seattle, are examples of sudden death in children treated with TCAs for psychiatric disorders (Varley CK, McClellan J, 1997). A boy, aged 9 years, died after 5 weeks treatment with desipramine, 100mg daily, for depression; cardiac arrest was preceded by a complaint of stomach pains followed by a convulsion. A boy, aged 7 years, died after treatment with imipramine 150 mg and thioridazine 25 mg for depression, oppositional defiance, and learning disorder; he collapsed and died in cardiac arrest after running several blocks home from school. Autopsies in both children failed to uncover any heart or brain abnormalities. The authors cite 5 additional reports since 1990 of sudden death in children treated with desipramine for psychiatric disorders.

Buproprion (Wellbutrin®) is a novel antidepressant, chemically unrelated to other agents, which blocks the uptake by neurons of the neurotransmitters, serotonin and norepinephrine. Although generally indicated for use in adults, the effectiveness of Wellbutrin in the treatment of ADHD in children has been demonstrated in several controlled studies (Simeon JG et al, 1986; Casat CD et al, 1987; Clay TH et al, 1988). Wellbutrin is usually well tolerated and is a useful alternative, when first line stimulant medications are ineffective or associated with serious side effects. It may also be indicated in patients with ADHD complicated by mood disorders. In one controlled study, comparing treatment with buproprion and methylphenidate in 15 children with ADHD, both drugs were effective, rating scales tending to favor MPH (Barrickman LL et al, 1995).

Buproprion has a slightly higher risk of causing or

exacerbating seizures than other antidepressants, especially in patients with a history of eating disorders. It should not be prescribed with other drugs known to lower the seizure threshold. Buproprion is not recommended in patients with a personal or family history of epilepsy or an abnormal EEG, unless seizures are controlled by antiepileptic medications.

Side effects of buproprion, also seen with methylphenidate and amphetamines, include an exacerbation of tics in children with comorbid ADHD and Tourette syndrome (Spencer T et al, 1993), and the occurrence of insomnia at the beginning of treatment. Tics and Tourette syndrome may be a contraindication to its use. Insomnia may be prevented by avoiding bedtime doses. Other occasional side effects in children include skin rash, swollen lips, nausea, increased appetite, tremor, and agitation (Casat, 1987; Clay, 1988; Dulcan MK, 1994).

Carbamazepine (Tegretol®) is an anticonvulsant, especially effective in complex partial and generalized tonic-clonic seizures. It also has some mood stabilizing properties. A review of several studies reporting the results of carbamazepine (CBZ) therapy for ADHD showed that 70% of patients were improved. Hyperactivity, impulsivity and distractibility were controlled following treatment with CBZ, and the longer the treatment the better the outcome.

In 3 placebo-controlled, double-blind studies, 71% of 53 patients treated with CBZ were benefited whereas only 26% of 52 receiving placebo showed improvements in attentiveness and behavior. The difference was significant. Side effects, mainly drowsiness and skin rash, occurred in 7% and 6% of patients, respectively (Silva RR et al, 1996).

CBZ may be a useful alternative therapy for ADHD, especially in patients with a history of epilepsy or with an abnormal electroencephalogram (EEG). My own review of the literature revealed that 70 to 80% of the patients with ADHD benefited by treatment with CBZ had abnormal EEGs. Most antiepileptic medications, including CBZ, may cause cognitive impairment and impulsivity in patients treated for epilepsy (Millichap JG, 1997). Treatment with CBZ must be monitored with measurements of drug levels, blood counts, and liver function tests.

Carbatrol®, a carbamazepine extended-release capsule, recently introduced, may be swallowed whole, or the contents sprinkled on food, for ease of administration. Like Tegretol-XR tablet form, Carbatrol is taken twice daily.

Q: Is it better to rely on well-tried stimulant medications in treating ADHD or turn to novel less-established remedies?

A: A number of alternative and less well-tried medications are sometimes prescribed for the treatment of ADHD. Ritalin® (methylphenidate) is the mainstay of the drug therapies available, its effectiveness and safety having been established for more than 30 years. Other stimulants, Dexedrine® and Adderal®, are also effective and are sometimes substituted, according to the preference of the physician or when Ritalin® has proven unsatisfactory. Antihypertensive agents, Catapres® (clonidine) and Tenex® (guanfacine), are indicated in children with ADHD complicated by tics or comorbid oppositional defiance and aggression, and the antidepressant agent, Wellbutrin® (buproprion) is of value in children with ADHD and comorbid mood disorders or those failing to respond to stimulants.

The tricyclic antidepressants are sometimes prescribed as second-line therapy for ADHD. However, the cardiovascular side effects, rarely resulting in fatalities, are a major concern, and careful monitoring and caution are essential. My personal preference is to rely on well-tried and safer remedies. Shakespeare's *Hamlet* has appropriate advice for doctors treating ADHD, given by Polonius to his son Laertes, and paraphrased as follows:

> *Those drugs thou hast, and their adoption tried,*
> *Grapple them to thy soul with hoops of steel;*
> *But do not dull thy palm with entertainment*
> *Of each new-hatch'd, unfledged remedy.*

REFERENCES

Abramowitz AJ, Dulcan MK et al. ADHD children's responses to stimulant medication and two intensities of a behavioral intervention. Behavior Modification 1992;16:193-203.

Ahmann PA et al. Placebo-controlled evaluation of Ritalin side effects. Pediatrics 1993;91:1101-1106.

Auci DL et al. Methylphenidate and the immune system (Letter to the editor). J Am Acad Child Adolesc Psychiatry 1997;36:1015-1016.

Barkley RA et al. Attention deficit disorder with and without hyperactivity: Clinical response to three dose levels of methylphenidate. Pediatrics 1991;87:519-531.

Barkley RA et al. Motor vehicle driving competencies and risks in teens and young adults with attention deficit hyperactivity disorder. Pediatrics 1996;98:1089-1095.

Barrickman LL et al. Buproprion versus methylphenidate in the treatment of attention-deficit hyperactivity disorder. J Am Acad Child Adolesc Psychiatry 1995;34:649-657.

Biederman J et al. Diagnostic continuity between child and adolescent ADHD. J Am Acad Child Adolesc Psychiatry 1998;37:305-313.

Bowen J et al. Stimulant medication and attention-deficit hyperactivity disorder. The child's perspective. AJDC 1991;145:291-295.

Bradley C. The behavior of children receiving Benzedrine. Am J Psychiatry 1937;94:577-585.

Bradley C. Benzedrine and Dexedrine in the treatment of children's behavior disorders. Pediatrics 1950;5:24-36.

Casat CD et al. A double-blind trial of buproprion in children with attention deficit disorder. Psychopharmacol Bull 1987;23:120-122.

Castellanos FX et al. Controlled stimulant treatment of ADHD and comorbid Tourette's syndrome: effects of stimulant and dose. J Am Acad Child Adolesc Psychiatry 1997;36:58.

Clay TH et al. Clinical and neuropsychological effects of the novel antidepressant buproprion. Psychopharmacol Bull 1988;24:143-148.

Conners CK, Eisenberg L. The effects of methylphenidate on symptomatology and learning in disturbed children. Am J Psychiatry 1963;120:458-464.

Denckla MB, Bemporad JR, MacKay MC. Tics following methylphenidate administration. JAMA 1976;235:1349-51.

Douglas VI et al. Do high doses of stimulants impair flexible thinking in attention-deficit hyperactivity disorder? J Am Acad Child Adolesc Psychiatry 1995;34:877-885.

Dulcan MK. Treatment of children and adolescents. In: RE Hales, SC Yodofsky, JA Talbott (Eds), The American Psychiatric

Press Textbook of Psychiatry, 2nd ed, Washington, DC, American Psychiatric Press, 1994, pp 1209-1250.

DuPaul GJ, Rapport MD. Does methylphenidate normalize the classroom performance of children with attention deficit disorder? J Am Acad Child Adolesc Psychiatry 1993;32:190-198.

Feeney DJ, Klykylo WM. Medication-induced seizures. (Letter to the editor). J Am Acad Child Adolesc Psychiatry 1997;36:1018-1019.

Feldman H et al. Methylphenidate in children with seizures and attention-deficit disorder. AJDC 1989;143:1081-1086.

Funk JB et al. Attention deficit hyperactivity disorder, creativity, and the effects of methylphenidate. Pediatrics 1993;91:816-819.

Gillberg C et al. Long-term stimulant treatment of children with attention-deficit hyperactivity disorder symptoms. Arch Gen Psychiatry 1997;54:857-864.

Goldman LS et al. Diagnosis and treatment of attention-deficit/hyperactivity disorder in children and adolescents. JAMA 1998;279:1100-1107.

Gross-Tsur V et al. Epilepsy and attention deficit hyperactivity disorder: Is methylphenidate safe and effective? J Pediatr 1997;130:670-674.

Handen BL et al. Prediction of response to methylphenidate among children with ADHD and mental retardation. J Am Acad Child Adolesc Psychiatry 1994;33:1185-1193.

Hochman JA et al. Exacerbation of autoimmune hepatitis: another hepatotoxic effect of pemoline therapy. Pediatrics 1998;101:106-108.

Jensen PS et al. Collaborative multimodal treatment study of children with ADHD. Arch Gen Psychiatry 1997;54:865-70.

Johnston C et al. Psychostimulant rebound in attention deficit disordered boys. J Am Acad Child Adolesc Psychiatry

1988;27:806-810.

Keuthen NJ et al. Retrospective review of treatment outcome for 63 patients with trichotillomania. Am J Psychiatry 1998;155:560-561.

Kouris S. Methylphenidate-induced obsessive-compulsiveness. J Am Acad Child Adolesc Psychiatry 1998;37:135.

Malhotra S, Santosh PJ. An open clinical trial of buspirone in children with attention-deficit/hyperactivity disorder. J Am Acad Child Adolesc Psychiatry 1998;37:364-371.

Mannuzza S et al. Adult psychiatric status of hyperactive boys grown up. Am J Psychiatry 1998;155:493-498.

McBride MC et al. Use of Ritalin in the hyperactive patient with seizures controlled by anticonvulsant drugs. Ann Neurol 1986;20:428.

Millichap MG. Locus of control in children with ADHD. Personal communication. 1998.

Millichap JG et al. Hyperkinetic behavior and learning disorders: III. Battery of neuropsychological tests in controlled trial of methylphenidate. Am J Dis Child 1968;116:235-244.

Millichap JG. Drugs in management of minimal brain dysfunction. Ann N Y Acad Sci 1973;205:321-334.

Millichap JG. (Ed). Learning Disabilities and Related Disorders: Facts and Current Issues. Chicago, Year Book Medical Publishers, 1977.

Millichap JG. Usage of CNS stimulants for ADHD by pediatric neurologists. Ped Neur Briefs 1996;10:65.

Millichap JG. Progress in Pediatric Neurology III. Chicago, PNB Publishers, 1997.

Millichap JG, Swisher CN. Ritalin-induced seizures in two children with ADHD. Ped Neur Briefs May 1997;11:38.

Millichap JG. Medication-induced seizures in ADHD. Ped Neur Briefs May 1997;11:63.

Musten LM et al. Effects of methylphenidate on preschool children with ADHD: cognitive and behavioral functions. J Am Acad Child Adolesc Psychiatry 1997;36:1407-1415.

Nolan EE, Gadow KD. Children with ADHD and tic disorder and their classmates: behavioral normalization with methylphenidate. J Am Acad Child Adolesc Psychiatry 1997;36:597-604.

O'Toole K, Abramowitz A, Morris R, Dulcan M. Effects of methylphenidate on attention and nonverbal learning in children with attention-deficit hyperactivity disorder. J Am Acad Child Adolesc Psychiatry 1997;36:531-538.

Rapport MD et al. Attention deficit disorder and methylphenidate: Normalization rates, clinical effectiveness, and response prediction in 76 children. J Am Acad Child Adolesc Psychiatry 1994;33:882-893.

Rapport MD, Denney C. Titrating methylphenidate in children with attention-deficit/hyperactivity disorder: Is body mass predictive of clinical response? J Am Acad Child Adolesc Psychiatry 1997;36:523-530.

Riggs PD. Approach to treatment of ADHD in adolescents with substance use disorders and conduct disorder. J Am Acad Child Adolesc Psychiatry 1998;37:331-332.

Rosh JR et al. Four cases of severe hepatotoxicity associated with pemoline: Possible autoimmune pathogenesis. Pediatrics 1998;101:921-923.

Safer D et al. Depression of growth in hyperactive children on stimulant drugs. N Engl J Med 1972;287:217.

Safer DJ et al. Increased methylphenidate usage for attention deficit disorder in the 1990s. Pediatrics 1996;98:1084-88.

Schachar RJ et al. Behavioral, situational, and temporal effects of treatment of ADHD with methylphenidate. J Am Acad Child Adolesc Psychiatry 1997;36:754-763.

Shevell M, Schreiber R. Pemoline-associated hepatic failure: a critical analysis of the literature. Pediatr Neurol 1997;16:14-16.

Silva RR et al. Carbamazepine use in children and adolescents with features of attention-deficit hyperactivity disorder: a meta-analysis. J Am Acad Child Adolesc Psychiatry 1996;35:352-358.

Simeon JG et al. Buproprion effects in attention deficit and conduct disorders. Can J Psych 1986;31:581-585.

Smith BH et al. Equivalent effects of stimulant treatment for attention-deficit hyperactivity disorder during childhood and adolescence. J Am Acad Child Adolesc Psychiatry 1998;378:314-321.

Spencer T et al. Buproprion exacerbates tics in children with attention deficit hyperactivity disorder and Tourette's syndrome. J Am Acad Child Adolesc Psychiatry 1993;32:211-214.

Spencer T et al. Pharmacotherapy of ADHD reviewed. J Am Acad Child Adolesc Psychiatry 1996;35:409-432.

Sprague R, Sleator E. Methylphenidate in hyperkinetic children: Differences in dose effects on learning and social behavior. Science 1977;198:1274-1276.

Stein MA et al. Methylphenidate dosing: twice daily versus three times daily. Pediatrics 1996;98:748-756.

Swanson JM et al. Analog classroom assessment of Adderal in children with ADHD. J Am Acad Child Adolesc Psychiatry May 1998;37:519-526.

Swartwood MO et al. Methylphenidate effects on EEG, behavior, and performance in boys with ADHD. Pediatr Neurol 1998;18:244-250.

Whalen CK, Henker B et al. Natural social behaviors in hyperactive children: Dose effects of methylphenidate. J Consult Clin Psychol 1987;55:187-193.

Whalen CK et al. Does stimulant medication improve the peer

status of hyperactive children? J Consult Clin Psychol 1989;57:5435-5449.

Wilens TE et al. Cardiovascular effects of therapeutic doses of tricyclic antidepressants in children and adolescents. J Am Acad Child Adolesc Psychiatry 1996;35:1491-1501.

CHAPTER 10

DIETS AND ALTERNATIVE CONTROVERSIAL THERAPIES

Various alternative therapies for ADHD have been offered as substitutes or supplements to medication and behavioral treatments. Some of these merit a trial in children unresponsive or showing toxic reactions to medications, and others appear to show little advantage except as a placebo. The evaluation of claims for therapies in a disorder such as ADHD, without a single, well-defined cause, is a scientific challenge, requiring controls and appropriate measurement techniques.

Subjective bias or prejudice may be excluded by use of a placebo (Latin for "I shall please") or control treatment and a double-blind trial. Both researchers and subjects treated are unaware of which patients are receiving active treatment or placebo. Unfortunately, remedies are often publicized before they have been subjected to rigorous scientific evaluation by recognized experts. Parents, in their efforts to find help, may be confused by enthusiastic claims for novel treatments and may be persuaded to try unproven remedies. Fortunately, most are without physical harm to the child, but many consume time, energy, and finances of the families involved.

Q: Why are parents sometimes convinced that scientifically unproven treatments are effective in their child?

A: There are two reasons why parents may be convinced of the value of a treatment when scientific study has failed to demonstrate effectiveness. First, the methods of scientific study using groups of children with ADHD may fail to recognize positive effects in individuals, and evaluations by teacher and parent questionnaires may not allow measurement of small responses. The scientific method may not be as smart as a mother's intuitive observations. A second reason for a parent's enthusiasm for a certain treatment is the so-called "Hawthorne effect."

In Hawthorne, California, a study of the effect of environmental lighting on workers' performance found that performance improved when the workplace lighting was either brightened or dimmed. Light intensity was not important but the change in environmental lighting had an indirect effect on work habits. Similarly, in a parent's evaluation of new treatments for ADHD, the specific type of therapy may be less important than the attention provided by the treatment.

An example of the failed scientific study in detection of behavioral changes observed by parents is the response of occasional children to sugar and chocolate deprivation and the omission of dyes in the diet. An example of the Hawthorne effect are the benefits that appear to follow sensory and perceptual motor training programs. Children may improve dramatically after enrollment in these exercises, but their effects on learning and behavior may be indirect (Hynd and Cohen, 1983).

Of all the alternative therapies proposed for the treatment of ADHD, diet and dietary supplements have demanded the most attention and caused frequent controversy. In the following question and answer sections, the separation of fact and fantasy about diet and behavior will be attempted by referral to the current scientific literature and results of controlled investigations.

Q: What are the various diets or diet supplements advocated in the treatment and prevention of ADHD and learning disorders?

A: A list of the dietary treatments proposed for ADHD and learning disorders includes the following:

- Sugar restricted diet.
- Additive and salicylate-free diet.
- Oligoantigenic diet.
- Ketogenic diet.
- Fatty acid supplements.
- Orthomolecular and megavitamin therapy.

For most of these diets and supplements, both positive and negative results have been reported. It may be concluded that a minority of children is responsive to one or another of the diets, but the demonstration of significant effects in a group of children as a whole may defy the available scientific method.

Q: What is the evidence for and against a sugar-restricted diet for ADHD?

A: FOR. Studies in favor of a sugar-restricted diet include the following:

At Colorado State University, 30 preschool children (20 boys and 10 girls, mean age 5 years 4 mos) and 15 elementary school children (6 boys and 9 girls, mean age 7yrs 2 mos) received a breakfast of high sucrose content (50 gm), low sucrose (6 gm), or aspartame (122 mg), randomly selected, 5 days on each, using a double-blind control design. On measures of cognitive function, girls made significantly less errors on a learning task performed 30 min following the low-sugar content breakfast when compared to the high-sugar meal, whereas boys were unaffected. On an Abbreviated Conners Teacher Rating Scale completed before lunch, both boys and girls were more active in behavior after the high sugar meal compared to a low sugar intake. Prior to the study, approximately 50% of the children were considered behaviorally sensitive to sugar, based on parent and teacher questionnaires (Rosen LA et al, 1988).

At the Children's Hospital, Washington, DC, the adverse effects of sugar in children with ADHD were demonstrated only if the challenge dose of sucrose was taken after a high carbohydrate breakfast. The hyperactive response could be prevented by a high protein breakfast (Conners CK, personal communication, 1987).

The beneficial and protective effects of a protein diet are correlated with neuroendocrine changes and blocking of serotonergic effects of sugar on behavior and attention. Diets low in protein and high in carbohydrates have been found to cause increased spontaneous activity in animal studies. For reviews of the effects of dietary nutrients and deficiencies on brain biochemistry and behavior, see Yehuda S (1986, 1987).

At the *Schneider Children's Hospital, New York,* the effects of sugar in a sample of young hyperactive boys with ADHD were similar to those observed by Conners. Inattention, measured by a continuous performance task, was increased following a sucrose drink given with a breakfast high in carbohdrate, but not after a drink containing aspartame (Wender EH, Solanto MV, 1991).

Inattentiveness may be benefited by the restriction of sucrose at the morning meal, by avoidance of a high carbohydrate breakfast, or by providing a protein containing balanced meal.

At *Yale University School of Medicine, New Haven, CT,* the immediate and delayed (3 - 5 hours) effects of a glucose load on plasma glucose and epinephrine levels were compared in 25 healthy children and 23 young adults. A late fall in plasma glucose (reactive hypoglycemia) stimulated a rise in epinephrine, twice as high in children compared to adults, and hypoglycemic symptoms (shakiness, sweating, weakness, or rapid pulse) occurred in children but not in adults. A measure of cognitive function by auditory evoked potentials (P300 amplitude), that was significantly reduced when glucose levels fell to 75 mg/dl in children, was preserved until the level fell to 54 mg/dl in adults (Jones TW et al, 1995).

Children are more vulverable to a glucose load and the effects of hypoglycemia on cognitive function and behavior than are adults. The avoidance of rapidly absorbed glucose or sucrose-containing foods in young children might prevent diet related exacerbations of ADHD. A balanced diet of protein, fat, and complex carbohydrates should limit a sudden fall in glucose levels after a meal, and should avoid symptoms related to the epinephrine hormonal response.

At the University of Pittsburgh School of Medicine, mild hypoglycemia (60 mg/dl) caused a significant decline in performance of a battery of cognitive tests in a study of adolescents with insulin-dependent diabetes mellitus, whereas hyperglycemia had no effect (Gschwend S et al, 1995).

This study in diabetics supports the theory that a delayed fall in blood sugar following a high sucrose load can have an adverse effect on learning. A sugar-restricted diet may benefit children with ADHD.

At Otto-von-Guericke University, Magdeburg, Germany, the effects of hypoglycemia on cognition were studied using event-related brain potential (ERP) measures and reaction times. Compared to base-line readings, measures of selective attention, choice of response and reaction time were delayed during hypoglycemia, and responses were slow to recover after normal blood sugar levels were restored. The frontal cortex, known to be involved in the control of attention, was more highly activated than other brain regions during acute hypoglycemia (Smid H et al, 1997).

This electrophysiological approach to the study of effects of sugar levels on learning also demonstrates an adverse effect of hypoglycemia, supporting a possible relation between sugar and symptoms of ADHD.

AGAINST. Studies failing to demonstrate either an adverse effect of sugar or a difference between sugar-containing and sugar-restricted meals were as follows:

At the University of Toronto, Ontario, Canada, the frequency of minor and gross motor behaviors, measured by "actometer" readings and video taped observations, was significantly less in 9-10 year-old normal children after the consumption of a sucrose drink than after a drink containing aspartame. Different responses might occur in ADHD children. Also in this study, measures of associative learning, arithmetic calculation, activity level, social interaction and mood were unaffected by a drink containing aspartame (Saravis S et al, 1990).

At Vanderbilt University, Nashville, TN, 25 normal preschool children (3 to 5 years of age) and 23 school-age children (6 to 10 years) described by their parents as sensitive to sugar received a diet high in sucrose or an aspartame substitute for three week periods. Measures of behavior and cognitive performance showed no significant differences between the groups. Neither sucrose nor aspartame caused a worsening of behavior or impairment of learning in normal or alleged sucrose-sensitive children (Wolraich ML et al, 1994).

It may still be argued that individual children are sensitive to sugar or aspartame but adverse effects are difficult to document by limited trial periods in children selected for specific studies.

PARTIALLY FOR AND AGAINST. Some studies provided conflicting results, as follows:

At the National Institute of Mental Health, Bethesda, MD, 18 boys, aged 2-6 years, rated by parents as "sugar responders," and 12 male playmates rated as "non responders" received single doses of sucrose, glucose, aspartame, or saccharine in a randomized, double-blind design. Parent and teacher ratings of activity levels and aggression failed to show differences between substances for either the alleged "responders" or "non responders." No parent differentiated between sugar and artificial sweetener trials. Whereas acute sugar loading did not increase aggression or activity in preschool children, the daily sucrose intake and total sugar consumption correlated with duration of aggression for the alleged sugar-responsive group (Krnesi MJP et al, 1987).

At the Schneider Children's Hospital, New York, boys with ADHD and oppositional disorder and age-matched control subjects received either sucrose or an aspartame drink with a breakfast high in carbohyrate. Measures of aggressive behavior were unchanged by either sucrose or aspartame, but inattention, measured by a continuous performance task, was exacerbated in the ADHD group following sugar, but not with aspartame (Wender EH, Solanto MV, 1991).

It follows that the avoidance of sucrose might benefit inattentiveness in the ADD child.

Q: Should aspartame and diet sodas be restricted in ADHD children?

A: The FDA and the manufacturer claim that aspartame (Nutrasweet®) and diet drinks are safe, except for children with phenylketonuria. Despite these claims, consumer groups and some scientists issue warnings of reported side effects and brain disorders related to the widespread ingestion of aspartame in dietary beverages and foods.

Researchers at the Departments of Psychiatry and Biostatistics, Washington University Medical School, St Louis, have proposed a link between the increasing rate of brain tumors and the introduction of aspartame in the diet in the 1980s (Olney JW et al, 1996). A review of earlier studies from equally prestigious universities, and published following peer review in recognized medical journals, has concluded that aspartame can precipitate migraine headaches and exacerbate EEG abnormalities in children with epilepsy (Millichap JG, 1991, 1994, 1997).

Despite the controversy over the validity of these reports and the lack of hard evidence of adverse effects on learning and behavior, aspartame ingestion in children with ADHD should probably be limited, pending a review of its safety by an unbiased panel of experts. The following are some recent reports of the effects of aspartame in normal and in ADHD children:

Studies failing to support a ban on aspartame in children with ADHD include reports from Schneider Children's Hospital, New York (Wender EH, Solanto MV, 1991), Vanderbilt University, Nashville, TN (Wolraich ML et al, 1994), and the University of Toronto, Ontario, Canada (Saravis S et al, 1990).

A study at Yale University School of Medicine, showing mixed results in 15 ADD children, found no significant differences between aspartame (single morning doses before school for 2 weeks) and placebo on various measures of cognition, behavior, and monoamine metabolism, but a significant increase in activity level following aspartame based on Teacher Ratings (Shaywitz BA et al, 1994). Until more evidence is available, specifically in ADHD children, Nutrasweet-containing drinks and foods should probably be restricted in the diets of children with ADHD, epilepsy, or headaches.

Q: What is the current medical opinion of the additive and salicylate-free diet in ADHD?

A: After sugar, additives and preservatives have attracted the interest of parents of children with ADHD more than most items in the diet. The Feingold additive-free diet was introduced in 1975, with the publication of a book entitled "Why Your Child is Hyperactive." Without documentation by controlled studies, the author claimed success in more than 50% of hyperactive children treated. The enthusiasm generated as a result of premature and widespread publicity stimulated the necessity for Federally organized and supported scientific trials.

Controlled studies in two major universities failed to provide convincing evidence for the efficiency of the additive-free diet to the extent claimed by Dr Feingold (Conners CK et al, 1976; Harley JP et al, 1978). Nevertheless, a small subset of younger pre-school children appeared to respond adversely to additives when presented as a challenge. It was concluded that an occasional child might react adversely to dyes and preservatives in the diet and might benefit from their elimination.

The interest in additives in relation to ADHD among parents and neurologists in the United States has waned, but in England, Europe, and Australia, the avoidance of foods containing additives is of widespread concern and their relation to behavior continues to be investigated. In a study of the prevalence of food additive intolerance in the UK, 7% of 18,000 respondents to questionnaires reported reactions to additives, and 10% had symptoms related to aspirin. A preponderance of additive-related behavioral and mood reactions occurred in children, boys more than girls (Young E et al, 1987).

At the Royal Children's Hospital, Victoria, Australia, of 55 hyperactive children included in a 6 week open trial of the Feingold diet, 47% showed a placebo response, and 25% were identified as likely reactors to additives (Rowe KS, 1988). In a larger group of 200 hyperactive children, 150 reported behavioral improvements on a diet free of synthetic colorings. A subsequent double-blind, placebo-controlled, 21 day challenge study of 34 suspected reactors identified 24 with a significant behavioral change that varied in severity with the dose of tartrazine synthetic colorings. Extreme irritability, restlessness and sleep disturbance rather than attention deficit were the common behavioral patterns associated with the ingestion of food colorings (Rowe KS, Rowe KJ, 1994).

The number of reactors to the synthetic dye, tartrazine, identified in this Australian study is significant and contrasts markedly with the isolated cases reported in earlier studies in the United States. Children with ADHD complicated by irritability, restlessness and sleep disturbance may be benefited by an additive-free diet. The strict DSM criteria for the diagnosis of ADHD and an inappropriate behavioral rating scale, omitting irritability and sleep disturbance, may have failed to identify some reactors to food additives in previous studies of the diet. In Australia, the Feingold hypothesis is still alive, and in the United States, further interest in the use of the additive free diet may be warranted (Millichap JG, 1993).

Q: What are the foods omitted and those

permitted in the additive-free diet for ADHD?

A: According to the Feingold diet, foods to be avoided included apples, grapes, luncheon meats, sausage, hot dogs, jams, gum, candies, gelatine, cake mixes, oleomargarine and ice creams, cold drinks and soda pop containing artificial flavors and coloring agents. Medicines containing aspirin were also excluded. Red and orange synthetic dyes were especially suspect, as well as preservatives, BHT and BHA, found in margarine, some breads and cake mixes, and potato chips.

Foods permitted included the following: grapefruit, pears, pineapple, and bananas; beef and lamb; plain bread, selected cereals, milk, eggs, home-made ice cream, and vitamins free of coloring. Labels and packages require checking to avoid offending additives, and a dietician should be consulted to ensure that the caloric content and food items are adequate for growth and metabolism. A parent wishing to follow this diet needs patience, perseverence, and the frequent monitoring by an understanding physician.

Q: What is the oligoantigenic diet for ADHD?

A: An oligoantigenic diet is one that eliminates all but a few known sensitizing food antigens or allergens. Foods most commonly found to be allergenic include cow's milk, cheese, wheat cereals, egg, chocolate, nuts, and citrus fruits. Skin tests for allergic reactivity to foods are unreliable, and elimination diets are required to test for specific food intolerances.

Lamb, potato, tapioca, carrots, peas, pears and sugar

are examples of hypoallergenic foods. After introduction of an oligoantigenic diet, improvements in behavior may be delayed for 10 days to two weeks. Individual foods are then added at weekly intervals and withdrawn if allergic symptoms are reproduced.

A combination of the antigen and additive free (AAF) diet is sometimes advised in suspected additive-reactive and allergy prone children (Millichap JG, 1986). If improvements in behavior are not evident after three to four weeks, alternative methods of treatment are considered.

At the Alberta Children's Hospital and Learning Center, Calagary, Canada, a 4 week trial of an AAF elimination diet in 24 hyperactive pre-school boys, aged 3.5 to 6 years, was associated with significant improvements in behavior in 42% and lesser improvements in 12%, when compared to baseline and placebo-control periods of observation (Kaplan BJ et al, 1989). The diet eliminated artificial colors and flavors, chocolate, monosodium glutamate, preservatives, and caffeine; it was low in sucrose, and dairy-free if an allergy to milk was suspected.

At the Universitatskinderklinik, Munchen, Germany, and the Allergy Unit, London, UK, a controlled trial of desensitization by intradermal food antigen injections found 16 of 20 hyperactive children became tolerant toward provoking foods, compared with 4 of 20 who received placebo injections. After desensitization, children with food-induced ADHD were able to eat the foods previously found to cause reactions, especially chocolate, colorings, cow milk, egg, citrus, wheat, nuts and cheese (Egger J et al, 1992).

These controlled studies lend support to the theory of food allergies and additives as a potential precipitating cause of ADHD in some patients.

Q: **What are the effects of the ketogenic diet for epilepsy and fatty acids on ADHD?**

A: Some children with epilepsy are also hyperactive, and a high-fat/low-carbohydrate (ketogenic) diet is occasionally used in treatment, particularly when seizures are resistant to antiepileptic drugs (AEDs). In addition to seizure control, an added benefit of the ketogenic diet is a noticeable improvement in hyperactive behavior, attentiveness, and cognitive abilities. With better seizure control, the doses of AEDs known to impair behavior and learning can often be reduced. For reviews of the effects and mechanism of the ketogenic diet, see Progress in Pediatric Neurology I and II (Millichap JG, 1991 and 1994).

Studies of fatty acid supplements in the treatment of children and adults with dyslexia have provided some interesting but conflicting preliminary results. Low serum levels of docosahexaenoic (DHA) and arachidonic acids are reported in hyperactive children with dyslexia, but treatment with supplements in the form of evening primrose oil had only modest and equivocal effects (Mitchell EA et al, 1987). In a later study in adults, improvements in dark adaptation and reading ability followed treatment of dyslexics with DHA supplements (Stordy BJ, 1995). These reports are anecdotal and the effects as yet unproven by controlled studies. Other fatty acid supplements of unproven efficacy include preparations of phosphatidylserine and choline.

Q: **What are the rationale and risks of "orthomolecular" and megavitamin therapy for ADHD and learning disorders?**

A: The terms orthomolecular psychiatry and megavitamin therapy are now used synonymously to describe a theory and treatment of mental illness. The term orthomolecular, very simply stated, means "right molecule." The concept was adopted by Nobel Prize winner, Dr Linus Pauling, in 1968. He proposed a treatment of mental disease, principally schizophrenia, using megadoses of niacin (vitamin B3), ascorbic acid (vitamin C), other vitamins, the minerals - zinc and manganese, and cereal-free diets. This combination of nutrients was thought to provide the optimum molecular environment for the mind. The treatment was subsequently advocated for children with hyperactivity, and for mental retardation and Down's syndrome (Cott A, 1972).

In my own practice, an open trial of Vitamin B complex (Becotin®) in ten children with ADHD failed to demonstrate effects on pre- and post-trial measures of behavior and psychological function. A double-blind controlled study was not considered warranted based on these preliminary results (Millichap JG, 1986).

Biological subgroups of children with autistic and hyperactive behavior may be amenable to treatment with megavitamins and minerals but, for the most part, practitioners of orthomolecular-megavitamin therapy have failed to convince colleagues of the validity of their claims. Furthermore, megadoses of some vitamins are not without danger. For example, pyridoxine (vitamin B6), in doses of 100 mg or above, can cause peripheral neuropathy if continued for prolonged periods (Millichap JG, 1997).

Q: What is the basis for mineral and trace element treatment of ADHD?

A: The theory of trace element and mineral deficiency as a cause of ADHD and learning disabilities was proposed on the basis of hair analyses and a report of lower than normal values for several minerals. Caution in the interpretation of hair analyses is important, since environmental and seasonal factors, age, sex and infection can affect mineral concentrations in hair samples, in addition to dietary factors (Millichap JG, 1991).

Trace elements such as zinc, copper, manganese, iron, selenium, copper, and fluorine can cause disease either as a result of a deficiency state or when consumption is in excess of normal requirements. Toxicity may result from food additives or adulteration, or from inadvised prescription or nonprescription medicines. The recognition of symptoms and signs of chronic, low-level trace element exposure is often difficult and the interactions between minerals are poorly understood (Millichap JG, 1993).

At the Dyslexia Institute, Staines, Middlesex, and the Hornsby Learning Centre, London, UK, an association between dyslexia and low concentrations of zinc in sweat analyses has been demonstrated in a study of 26 children, aged 6 to 14 years, attending for treatment. Hair analyses showed no differences in zinc concentrations but higher concentrations of copper, lead and cadmium were present, when compared to control normal readers. Measurement of zinc in sweat was a more useful guide to clinical zinc deficiency than hair or serum analyses. The authors theorize that zinc deficiency in the mother might predispose to developmental dyslexia (Grant ECG et al, 1988).

Mineral analyses, especially zinc, may be warranted in children with learning disorders, but the need for adequate controls and appropriate specimen collection is emphasized. Treatment based on inaccurate measurement techniques may lead to toxicity.

Q: What is the rationale for biofeedback techniques in the treatment of ADHD?

A: Children with hyperactive behavior and attention deficits have a high incidence of abnormal EEGs, and poorly organized alpha-wave activity in the occipital leads is a common finding. Experiments have indicated that patients can control their alpha-wave activity, and a high production of alpha waves at 8-14 Hz may be associated with mental alertness and physical relaxation. This is the basis for alpha-wave conditioning via biofeedback techniques in the treatment of ADHD. The treatment requires subject collaboration and, except in adolescents and adults, impractical as an office therapy.

Q: Is there any scientific support for optometric visual training in dyslexia and learning disabilities?

A: Abnormalities of eye movements, tracking, and visual fixations are reported as characteristic of dyslexics. Optometric training techniques employed by some optometrists to treat dyslexia and other learning disabilities include a program of eye exercises designed to facilitate smooth and synchronized eye movements, special colored lenses, and visual-spatial and coordination exercises. In 1972, a joint statement critical of the optometric approach was published by the American Academies of Pediatrics and Ophthalmology, citing lack of scientific evidence to support the claims of success. Despite this word of caution, many parents are persuaded to enroll their children in optometric training programs, trusting that science may someday discover a plausible explanation for the benefits reported.

At the Departments of Biology, Electrical Engineering, and Computer Science, Massachusetts Institute of Technology, Cambridge, MA, researchers collaborated in an investigation of the peripheral and foveal (central) vision of 5 dyslexic adult subjects compared to 5 normal readers. Two letters, one at the fixation point and one at the periphery, at varying distances apart, were presented simultaneously and the scores for the correct identification of the single peripheral letters in the two groups were compared.

Normal readers and dyslexic subjects scored differently on this visual test. With letters briefly presented at or near the central fixation point, the scores of normal readers were higher, whereas dyslexic subjects were better at the correct identification of letters in the peripheral field of vision. After a 4 month program of exercises involving visual spatial organization and eye-hand coordination, together with a simple device to utilize the dyslexic's optimal peripheral vision, the performance of severe dyslexic subjects on reading tests showed improvements up to a tenth grade level.

Researchers conclude that an interaction between central and peripheral vision in dyslexics diminishes the normal ability to read using the central (foveal) field of vision. Dyslexics mask or suppress letter discrimination in the central field and are able to identify letters better in the peripheral field. They should be taught to read by use of their peripheral vision (Geiger G, Lettvin JY, 1987).

If this intriguing experiment and conclusion can be reproduced in children, the results lend support to the potential benefits of optometric training. Alternative explanations for the findings might be a change in attention and cortical visual organization peculiar to dyslexic subjects. However, the study offers a simple and practical method of treatment for dyslexia that warrants further research.

Q: What   is   vestibular   and   sensory integrative   therapy   for   ADHD?

A: Sensory integrative therapy employed by occupational therapists is based on a theory, first proposed by Ayres (1978, 1981), and outlined in Lerner J (1985), that perception and learning are dependent on brain stem function and organization and balance of auditory, visual, and tactile processes. An inadequate sensory integration in the brain stem is postulated in children with learning disabilities, because of immature postural reactions, poor eye muscle control, and impaired visual orientation and sound perception. Scientific support for impaired sensory integration and touch perception in children with ADHD is presented by researchers in Israel.

At   the   Hebrew   University,   Jerusalem,   Israel, somatosensory evoked potentials (SEP) and tactile function were tested in 49 ADHD children and 49 controls. ADHD children performed poorly on tactile perception tests, including finger identification, recognition of numbers traced on the palms, localization of touch stimuli, form perception, and joint movement. The SEP central components were larger in amplitude in ADHD children compared to controls, supporting the theory of brain cell hyperactivity in ADHD (Parush S et al, 1997).

In models of therapy based on these concepts, vestibular, postural and tactile stimulation is thought to improve auditory processing and to benefit auditory language disorders and visual perceptual functioning. The vestibular system is stimulated by swinging, spinning, and rolling. Posture and motor development are trained by balance and muscle coordination exercises. The tactile system is stimulated through touching and rubbing skin surfaces. Occupational therapy involving tactile stimulation may lead to improved sensory integration and accelerated academic achievement.

Q: What is central auditory evaluation and training and when is it indicated in ADHD?

A: Central auditory evaluation consists of the standard puretone and speech audiometry or hearing tests together with special tests that require the identification of signals distorted by electronic filtering or presented in competition with speech or noise signals. Information regarding attention, decoding, and planning of auditory processing is evaluated (Jeanane M Ferre PhD, Oak Park, IL, personal communication).

In children with specific language and learning

disabilities, scores on dichotic listening tasks are impaired, suggesting a lack of ability to integrate auditory and non auditory information. Pitch discrimination and auditory pattern recognition skills may be affected, a function of impaired integration of the two brain hemispheres. Intersensory integration skills measured by competing messages in the two ears may be impaired in children with auditory-visual integration weakness. Excessive reversals are common with integrative central auditory deficits.

The integration of multiple auditory-language and/or intersensory information is necessary for sight word recognition and spelling. Weakness in these central auditory skills may adversely affect the ability to associate sounds and symbols, a skill needed for reading, spelling, writing, language and communication.

Methods of remediation of central auditory dysfunction are designed to aid integration and organization of material, using verbal rehearsal and visualization, and word association. Playing a musical instrument has been shown to enhance auditory and visual-spatial integration skills and to improve academic achievement.

Children with ADHD occasionally complain of dizziness or vertigo. A referral to an otolaryngologist or neuro-otologist may uncover a dysfunction of the peripheral and/or central vestibular function. Abnormalities of the electronystagmogram (ENG) and brain stem auditory evoked responses (BAER) are indications for a central auditory evaluation. Treatment for a central auditory dysfunction can benefit learning and language disabilities associated with ADHD.

Q: What is the scientific basis for music in facilitating learning?

A: The perception of music is a complex neurocognitive process involving various neural networks, with some anatomical specificity for the different basic auditory components of music (rhythm, pitch, timbre, and melody). Furthermore, visual cognitive imagery appears to be involved in pitch appreciation. Playing a musical instrument requires the functional integration of both brain hemispheres in addition to finger dexterity and coordination. As my violin teacher, Dr Marvin Ziporyn, correctly comments when I err on pitch of a chromatic scale, "It's all in the head, not in the fingers!"

At the Wellcome Department of Cognitive Neurology, Institute of Neurology, London, the cerebral functional anatomy of music appreciation was determined in six young, healthy, musically naive, right handed subjects, using a high resolution PET scanner and oxygen-15 labelled water. Four activation tasks on the same auditory material, consisting of 30 sequences of notes on tapes, were used: 1) identification/familiarity with tunes; 2) attention to pitch task; 3) timbre task; and 4) rhythm task.

Familiarity and recognition of tunes, and the *rhythm* task caused activation mainly in the left hemisphere, whereas the *timbre* task activated the right hemisphere. In contrast to previous studies in brain damaged subjects, *pitch* processing caused activation of the left hemisphere, in proximity to primary visual areas, and reflecting a visual mental imagery (Platel H et al, 1997).

At the Department of Physics, University of California, Irvine, the positive effects of music on spatial-temporal reasoning was demonstrated in college students by a special analysis of electroencephalographic recordings. Right frontal and left hemisphere EEG activity was induced by listening to 10 minutes of Mozart (Sonata for Two Pianos in D Major), and enhancement of spatial-temporal reasoning was carried over in 3 of 7 subjects. Relaxation tapes and minimalist music had no effect (Sarnthein J et al, 1998).

In their sophisticated scanning procedure, Platel, Frackowiak and coworkers have demonstrated the functional independence of sub-components of musical expression. The left hemisphere is dominant for rhythm, tune recognition, and pitch perception, while the right hemisphere is involved in timbre or quality of tone perception. The differentiation of pitch requires not only auditory but visual interpretation and mental imagery. Listening to Mozart enhances cortical cerebral activity used in spatial-temporal reasoning.

The positive effects on learning of listening to music and playing an instrument are corroborated by neuroanatomical and electrophysiological studies. Involvement in music can be recommended to children with ADHD and learning diasabilities.

REFERENCES

Ayres A. Sensory integration and the child. Los Angeles, Western Psychological Services, 1981.

Conners CK et al. Food additives and hyperkinesis. A controlled double-blind experiment. Pediatrics 1976;58:154-166.

Conners CK et al. The effects of sucrose on children with

attention deficit, In: Diet and Behavior. Lubbock, Texas Tech Univ Press, 1984.

Cott A. Megavitamins: The orthomolecular approach to behavioral disorders and learning disabilities. Academic Therapy 1972;7:245.

Egger J et al. Controlled trial of hyposensitization in children with food-induced hyperkinetic syndrome. Lancet 1992;339:1150-1153.

Feingold BF. Why Your Child is Hyperactive. New York, Random House, 1975.

Grant ECG et al. Zinc deficiency in children with dyslexia: concentrations of zinc and other minerals in sweat and hair. BMJ 1988;296:607-609.

Gschwend S et al. Effects of acute hyperglycemia on mental efficiency and counterregulatory hormones in adolescents with insulin-dependent diabetes mellitus. J Pediatr 1995;126:178-184.

Harley JP et al. Hyperkinesis and food additives: Testing the Feingold hypothesis. Pediatrics 1978;61:818-828.

Harley JP et al. Synthetic food colors and hyperactivity in children. Double-blind challenge experiment. Pediatrics 1978;62:975-983.

Hynd G, Cohen M. Dyslexia. Neuropsychological Theory, Research, and Clinical Differentiations. New York, Grune and Stratton, 1983.

Jones TW et al. Enhanced adrenomedullary response and increased susceptibility to neuroglycopenia: Mechanisms underlying the adverse effects of sugar ingestion in healthy children. J Pediatr 1995;126:171-177.

Kaplan BJ et al. Dietary replacement in preschool-aged hyperactive boys. Pediatrics 1989;83:7-17.

Krnesi MJP et al. Effects of sugar and aspartame on aggression and activity in children. Am J Psychiatry 1987;144:1487-

1490.

Lerner J. Learning Disabilities. Theories, Diagnosis, and Teaching Strategies. 4th Ed. Boston, Houghton Mifflin, 1985.

Millichap JG. Nutrition, Diet, and Your Child's Behavior. Springfield, IL, Charles C Thomas, 1986.

Millichap JG. Environmental Poisons in Our Food. Chicago, PNB Publishers, 1993.

Millichap JG. Progress in Pediatric Neurology I, II, & III. Chicago, PNB Publishers, 1991, 1994, & 1997.

Mitchell EA et al. Clinical characteristics and serum essential fatty acid levels in hyperactive children. Clin Pediatr 1987;26:406-411.

Olney JW et al. Increasing brain tumor rates: is there a link to aspartame? J Neuropathol Exp Neurol 1996;55:1115-1123.

Parush S et al. Somatosensory functioning in children with attention deficit hyperactivity disorder. Dev Med Child Neurol 1997;39:464-468.

Pauling L. Orthomolecular psychiatry. Science 1968;160:265.

Platel H et al. The structural components of music perception. A functional anatomical study. Brain 1997;120:229-243.

Rosen LA et al. Effects of sugar (sucrose) on children's behavior. J Consulting Clin Psychol 1988;56:583-589.

Rowe KS. Synthetic food colourings and 'hyperactivity': A double-blind crossover study. Aust Pediatr 1988;24:143-147.

Rowe KS, Rowe KJ. Synthetic food coloring and behavior: a dose response effect in a double-blind, placebo-controlled, repeated-measures study. J Pediatr 1994;125:691-698.

Saravis S et al. Aspartame: effects on learning, behavior and mood. Pediatrics 1990;86:75-83.

Sarnthein J et al. Persistent patterns of brain activity: An EEG coherence study of the positive effect of music on spatial-temporal reasoning. Neurol Res 1998;19:107-116.

Shaywitz BA et al. Aspartame, behavior, and cognitive function in children with attention deficit disorder. Pediatrics 1994;93:70-75.

Smid HGOM et al. Differentiation of hypoglycemia induced cognitive impairments. An electrophysiological approach. Brain 1997;120:1041-1056.

Stordy BJ. Benefit of docosahexaenoic acid supplements to dark adaptation in dyslexics. Lancet 1995;346:385.

Wender EH, Solanto MV. Effects of sugar on aggressive and inattentive behavior in children with attention deficit disorder with hyperactivity and normal children. Pediatrics 1991;88:960-966.

Wolraich ML et al. Behavior and cognitive performance of children unaffected by sucrose or aspartame. N Engl J Med 1994;330:301-307.

Yehuda S. Brain biochemistry and behavior. Nutrition Reviews, Suppl, May 1986;44:1-250.

Yehuda S. Brain biochemistry and behavior. Intern J Neuroscience 1987;35:21-36.

Young E et al. Prevalence of food additive intolerance in the UK. JRSM 1987;21:241-247.

CHAPTER 11

PROGNOSIS AND PREVENTION

"What is the outcome for my child when he or she grows up?" is a frequent question asked by parents of ADHD children. "Will he outgrow the ADHD?" "Will he need continued treatment with stimulant medication into adulthood?" "Is there an increased risk of drug abuse in adults with a history of childhood ADHD?" Some of the answers to these questions remain controversial, the outcome being influenced by complicating comorbid disorders and other factors.

Patients referred and treated in a neurology clinic for ADD may have less frequent comorbid disorders and a better outcome than those referred to psychiatry because of prominent symptoms of oppositional and conduct disorders. Many factors, including the cause, severity of symptoms, sex, socio-economic status, intelligence, learning disabilities, quality of education, parental care and emotional climate of the home, as well as medical treatment can influence the outcome. The following answers to questions are derived from group studies, and may not always apply in the prognosis of an individual child.

Q: Can I expect my child to outgrow the ADHD?

A: Medical opinion has changed regarding the outcome of childhood ADHD. Formerly, most pediatricians reassured parents by predicting that hyperactivity would resolve after 12 years of age. Currently, most experts favor a more quarded prognosis, with symptoms persisting to some degree in approximately 50% of ADHD children as they approach adulthood (Barkley RA, 1990). The majority make adjustments for their symptoms, but some experience continuing difficulties requiring treatment, especially those with comorbid psychiatric disorders. Even among psychiatrists, however, opinions vary regarding outcome, a recent study finding that children with uncomplicated ADHD may "outgrow" the disorder.

At the Long Island Jewish Medical Center, New Hyde Park, NY, 85 hyperactive boys with ADHD, referred at an average age of 7 years, were evaluated by psychiatric interview at a mean age of 24 years. ADHD had resolved, only 4% having continuing symptoms. Compared to controls, childhood ADHD subjects were at greater risk of developing antisocial personality disorder and nonalcohol substance abuse (12% versus 3%) as adults. Mood disorders in 4% and anxiety disorders in 2% were not more prevalent than in controls (Mannuzza S et al, 1998).

Risk factors for persistence of ADHD into adolescence include: 1) a genetic familial history of ADHD; 2) exposure to environmental psychosocial adversity and parent conflict; and 3) comorbidity with conduct, mood and anxiety disorders (Biederman J et al, 1996). Risk factors for predicting adult outcome are similar to those for adolescence and also include the following: 1) childhood intelligence estimates; 2) childhood hyperactivity and aggression; 3) child-rearing practices and emotional state of parents; and 4) socio-economic status (Weiss G, Hechtman L, 1986).

Q: What are the symptoms of ADHD in adults?

A: Problems with college education, occupation, or family and social relationships may prompt an adult with ADHD to consult a psychologist or psychiatrist. Common presenting complaints include the foiowing:

• Failure to complete college education because of inability to focus on assignments, impaired concentration, and distractibility.

• Frequent job changes because of poor performance, forgetfulness, and lack of organization.

• Poor social and spousal relationships because of quick temper, impulsiveness, low frustration tolerance, and low self-esteem.

Therapy and counselling can help, but a correct psychiatric diagnosis is essential before specific medication is prescribed. The risk of substance abuse is higher in adults, and buproprion (Wellbutrin) may be a safer choice than amphetamines or methylphenidate.

Samples of hyperactive children followed into adulthood have been examined for psychiatric complications, academic achievement, antisocial behavior, problems with employment, and social skills (Weiss G, Hechtman L, 1986; Barkley RA, 1990). Compared to controls, children with ADHD are more likely as adults to experience problems in one or all of these areas of functioning. With optimal management, however, the majority make satisfactory adult adjustments and compensations.

The best outcome appears to be associated with milder ADHD symptoms and higher IQ in childhood, together with well-adjusted parents and a stable family environment. The long-term benefits of stimulant medication on outcome have been demonstrated in one controlled study (Gillberg C et al, 1997), and a collaborative multimodal treatment study is in progress (Jensen PS et al, 1997).

Q: Does stimulant usage in childhood lead to an increased risk of substance or drug abuse among adolescents and adults with ADHD?

A: Children taking methylphenidate or other stimulant medication for ADHD do not appear to abuse stimulants in adolescence or adulthood. In fact, most children will express a desire to discontinue medication as early as possible. Media reports of abuse of stimulants among high school students have involved non-ADHD subjects with potential drug addiction.

Whereas stimulant therapy does not lead to substance use or abuse, the symptoms of ADHD do predispose to increased cigarette smoking and a tendency to alcohol use during adolescence, especially in those with comorbid disorders. Adolescents with ADHD complicated by conduct disorders are two to five times more likely to abuse cigarettes, alcohol, and also marijuana than hyperactives without CD or normal adolescents (Gittelman R et al, 1985; Barkley RA, 1990).

Children with ADHD referred to a psychiatric clinic are at increased risk of developing antisocial personality and nonalcoholic substance abuse disorders as grown ups. Substance abuse, mainly marijuana, in adults with a history of ADHD has been reported in 40% of patients with persistent symptoms of ADHD (Biederman J et al, 1995), and in 12% of those who have "outgrown" the ADHD by 24 years of age (Mannuzza S et al, 1998). Control subjects followed from childhood to 24 years showed a 4% incidence of substance abuse.

Antisocial personality, mood and anxiety disorders increase the risk of substance use and abuse, independent of ADHD. The preferred drugs of abuse are no different among ADHD adults and non-ADHD control subjects, and ADHD patients show no predilection for stimulant abuse. Nonetheless, adult ADHD is often a self-diagnosed condition, and an excuse for job failure, divorce, and spousal abuse. Psychoactive substance use disorder is commonly associated with adult ADHD, and stimulant medication should be used with caution (Shaffer D, 1994).

Q: What are the indications of a good prognosis in childhood ADHD?

A: A favorable outcome, high school graduation, and prospects of a college education might be expected in ADHD children with the following criteria:

• An average or above average IQ.

• Perceptual problems restricted to visual or visuo-motor dysfunctions, and without serious learning disorders.

• Absence of comorbid oppositional and especially, conduct disorders.

• Rapid and sustained response to stimulant medication, alleviating hyperactivity and improving academic achievement and perceptual function.

• Early psychological diagnosis and appropriate remedial education accommodations.

• Well-structured school and supportive home environments that lessen distractibility and improve attention span.

• Understanding parents and teachers who provide successful experiences and encouragement and avoid excessive criticism, bolstering self-confidence and leading to a healthy social and emotional development.

Q: When is the prognosis guarded or poor?

A: A favorable outcome is less likely in children with the following complications of ADHD:

• A persistently low average or borderline IQ,
• Global perceptual deficits, auditory and visual.
• Severe dyslexia or other learning disability.
• Poor response or intolerance to stimulant medications.
• Delayed psychological evaluation, and inadequate learning accommodations in school.
• Comorbid oppositional and conduct disorders, impervious to psychotherapeutic intervention.

Q: Why is it difficult to predict the outcome of ADHD?

A: ADHD is a heterogeneous syndrome, diverse in etiology and clinical manifestations. Both hereditary and environmental factors are important in the cause and outcome, but generally a specific cause is undetermined or idiopathic. Treatment is symptomatic and multimodal, involving parent, teacher, psychologist, and physician. For the majority, there is no simple or fast cure, and the outcome is determined by a variety of criteria. Studies directed to a more homogeneous cluster of symptoms and signs might lead to closer etiologic diagnoses and more accurate prediction of prognosis.

Q: What preventive measures might be indicated based on known potential causes of ADHD?

A: Several presumptive environmental causes have been linked to ADHD, and the following preventive measures are appropriate:

• Optimal medical attention and nutrition during pregnancy.

• Maternal avoidance of alcohol, nicotine, and drug use, especially cocaine, during pregnancy, birth, and breast feeding.

• Optimal obstetric care and avoidance of brain damage from anoxia and premature birth.

• Prompt pediatric attention to neonatal jaundice, hypoglycemia, febrile illness, convulsions, and thyroid dysfunction.

• Testing and treatment for lead exposure and poisoning in early childhood.

• Educational programs for the prevention of head

injuries, accidental drug ingestion, and lead and other poisonings.

• Well-structured and healthy emotional home environment.

• Optimal teacher-pupil ratio in small classrooms to lessen distractibility and facilitate learning.

REFERENCES

Barkley RA. Attention-Deficit Hyperactivity Disorder: A Handbook for Diagnosis and Treatment. New York, Guildford Press, 1990.

Biederman J et al. Psychoactive substance use disorders in adults with attention deficit hyperactivity disorder (ADHD): effects of ADHD and comorbidity. Am J Psychiatry 1995;152:1652-1658.

Biederman J et al. Predictors of persistence and remission of ADHD into adolescence: results from a four-year prospective follow-up study. J Am Acad Child Adolesc Psychiatry 1996;35:343-351.

Gillberg C et al. Long-term stimulant treatment of children with attention-deficit hyperactivity disorder symptoms. Arch Gen Psychiatry 1997;54:857-864.

Gittelman R et al. Hyperactive boys almost grown up. Arch Gen Psychiatry 1985;42:937-947.

Jensen PS et al. A collaborative multimodal treatment study of children with ADHD. Arch Gen Psychiatry 1997;54:865-70.

Mannuzza S et al. Adult psychiatric status of hyperactive boys grown up. Am J Psychiatry 1998;155:493-498.

Shaffer D. ADHD in adults. An editorial. Am J Psychiatry 1994;151:633-638.

Weiss G, Hechtman L. Hyperactive Children Grown Up. New York, Guidford Press, 1986.

CHAPTER 12

MANAGEMENT ROLES AND RESEARCH GOALS

The child with ADHD benefits from parental care and understanding, a teacher's attention to special educational needs, the psychologist's evaluation and behavior counselling, and a physician's diagnostic skill and medical treatment. Each has an important role in the multimodal management of the problem.

Q: What is the parent's role in the management of the child with ADHD?

A: The early recognition and optimal management of ADHD may be dependent on the education of the parent in the presenting symptoms and the value of various treatments available for ADHD. The following suggestions are offered regarding a parent's role in the management of ADHD:

• Be alert to the possible development of the syndrome in a young child if a family member has ADHD, the birth is complicated by anoxia or injury, or the early milestones of development are delayed.

• Learn about the early manifestations of ADHD, and consult a physician regarding the necessity for neurological or psychiatric investigations and treatment.

• Obtain a preschool evaluation to determine the correct educational placement and program.

• Consult a psychologist if a learning disability is likely.

• Provide a stable home environment and healthy emotional climate.

• Embrace recommended therapies of proven value used conservatively, and be cautious in acceptance of new and unofficial remedies.

• Join a local parent organization such as CHADD, to keep informed of recent developments and advances in the medical, educational, psychological, and legal fields related to ADHD.

Q: What is the teacher's role?

A: • Teachers should be aware of the symptoms and signs of ADHD and alert the parent and physician to the early recognition of the syndrome at preschool or kindergarten levels.

• Optimum programs of remedial education and academic accommodations should be provided to meet a child's individual needs, and based on results of achievement tests and psychological evaluations.

• A teacher's observations and reports regarding a child's response to medications and other therapies are of help to the physician in monitoring progress, and also the recognition of potential side effects of drugs.

Q: What is the role of the psychologist?

A: • The psychologist provides an evaluation of cognitive and behavioral functioning, using quantitative tests of intelligence, reading readiness and ability, arithmetical skills, visual-motor and auditory perception, and ratings of hyperactivity-impulsivity and inattentiveness. Comorbid oppositional, conduct, anxiety, and depressive disorders are also assessed.

The psychologist's report is essential to the teacher in determining the correct school placement and remedial program of education, and for the physician's evaluation of the diagnosis and optimal medical treatment.

• A psychologist may be the first to recognize absence seizures in a child who "daydreams" during an examination. By alerting the parent and physician to a potential seizure disorder, an electroencephalogram is expedited and the diagnosis and treatment facilitated. Frequent absence or partial complex seizures may sometimes masquerade as a learning disorder. Tics and obsessive compulsive disorders are often first recognized and reported by an alert psychologist.

• Family counselling and behavior modification, important in the multimodal treatment approach to ADHD, are provided by the psychologist.

• Psychologists are not usually responsible for the prescription of drugs, but their knowledge and expertise in psychopharmacology is valuable to the patient and physician in determining the optimal type and amount of medication required in the individual patient.

• Investigational psychologists have been responsible for much of the behavioral, psychopharmacological, and diet-related research in children with ADHD. Their knowledge of statistical analyses and controlled studies have expanded our scientific understanding and acceptance of treatments and outcome of ADHD. The psychologist's close collaboration with neurologist and psychiatrist is an invaluable asset to the multimodal management team.

Q: What is the physician's role in research and improved management of the child with ADHD?

A: A number of medical disciplines are involved in the investigation of the causes, diagnostic criteria, and treatments for ADHD.

• Geneticists advance their twin and other studies of hereditary aspects of ADHD, leading to the possible definition of an underlying gene abnormality.

• Pediatric neurologists in collaboration with neuroradiologists are pursuing the MRI volumetric analyses, PET and other brain imaging studies to further define a neuroanatomical basis for ADHD.

• Electrophysiologists are investigating changes in the EEG and evoked potentials during task performance.

• Neurochemists are pursuing the role of

neurotransmitters in the cause of ADHD.

• Psychiatrists are constantly changing and refining the symptomatic diagnostic criteria for ADHD and its various subtypes and comorbid disorders.

• Psychopharmacologists are extending trials of methylphenidate and other drugs, observing longterm effects and side effects. The recent introduction of a novel amphetamine, Adderal®, and the demonstration of effectiveness of the antidepressant, Wellbutrin®, may prove useful additions to medical therapy of ADHD.

• Allergists, mainly in the UK, Europe and Australia, are further investigating the role of diet and food additives in the cause of ADHD.

• Toxicologists and epidemiologists continue research in the effect of lead and other environmental poisons on cognition and behavior of children, the frequency of ADHD cases and their distribution.

• Endocrinologists unravel the role of thyroid dysfunction as an infrequent associated factor in ADHD.

• The possible influence of viral infections during pregnancy and early childhood has received some attention from epidemiologists. A seasonal variation in the birth patterns of children who develop ADHD, with peaks in September and winter months, might support a first-trimester or neonatal viral exposure. Historically, one of the first references to a hyperactive child syndrome was a sequel to the world war 1 influenza epidemic and encephalitis lethargica.

In reviewing the world medical literature monthly, as editor of the journal, "Pediatric Neurology Briefs," I am impressed with the volume of research and publications on ADHD. The classification of symptoms, diagnostic criteria, comorbid disorders, MRI studies, and trials of stimulant medications are the principal interests of investigators. Further work on the etiology of ADHD and the development of more specific therapies should be addressed.

REFERENCES

Millichap JG. Pediatric Neurology Briefs Vols. 1-12. Chicago, PNB Publishers, 1987-98.
Millichap JG. Ed. Progress in Pediatric Neurology I, II, & III. Chicago, PNB Publishers, 1991, 1994, 1997.

INDEX

SOME EARLY REVIEWS

"A thorough and understandable explanation of Attention Deficit Hyperactivity Disorder" Martha B. Denckla, M.D., Professor of Neurology, Pediatrics, and Psychiatry, Johns Hopkins University School of Medicine.

"A most scholarly work and doubly appealing. For pediatricians and pediatric neurologists, it is authoritative.. For parents and teachers, it is a very clear exposition..easily understood by informed lay-persons or professionals. The book is extremely well referenced." Dr John Wilson, F.R.C.P., Pediatric Neurologist, Great Ormond Street Hospital, London, UK.

"It's a great source of reference." Margaret O'Flynn, M.D., Professor of Pediatrics, Northwestern University Medical School, Children's Memorial Hosp, Chicago.

"This is by far the most unbiased ADD book I've read. It has answers to every possible question one might have." Barbara L. Pavoni, President, CH.A.D.D. Chapter, Chicago.

"Dr Millichap has written a superb book for all those concerned, either professionally or personally, with children, adolescents, and even adults" with ADHD. N

"Re / *resh* and *l* *l in* the *r* *pedi* *Jour*

frien *lled* *stud* *pedi* *Toure*

phys *and* *libra* *ealth*

pare *Chica*